BURTON CONSTABLE HALL

A Century of Patronage

by Ivan and Elisabeth Hall

with additional material by
A.G. Credland and M.J. Boyd

Hull City Museums and Art Galleries
and Hutton Press
1991

Published by Hull City Museums and Art Galleries

and the Hutton Press Ltd.
130 Canada Drive, Cherry Burton, Beverley
East Yorkshire HU17 7SB

Typeset and printed by
Image Colourprint Ltd.,
Anlaby, Hull.

ISBN 1 872167 22 5

CONTENTS

Preface 4

Foreword 5

Acknowledgements 6

Introduction 7

Family tree of the Constables of Burton Constable (A.G.C.) 9

Chapter One - The Constable Inheritance 1718-1870 (I.H.) 11

Chapter Two - Architectural development of Burton Constable Hall, (I.H.) 16

Chapter Three - William Constable - his ideas and ideals (I.H.) 19

Chapter Four - The Cabinet of scientific instruments (E.H.) 25

Chapter Five - Natural History - The Herbarium (E.H.) 33

Chapter Six - William Constable's 'Fossil Cabinet' (M.J.B.) 42

Chapter Seven - William Constable's Zoological collection (M.J.B. and E.H.) 48

Chapter Eight - The gun cabinet and the Wallis workshop (A.G.C.) 54

Chapter Nine - The Wallis museum, its inspirations and contemporaries (A.G.C.) 61

Chapter Ten - Constable the improver - the creation of a landscape garden (E.H.) 68

Chapter Eleven - The Library (E.H.) 72

Chapter Twelve - A century of Constable patronage (I.H.) 75

Chapter Thirteen - The Burton Constable Whale (A.G.C.) 81

Chapter Fourteen - Sir Clifford Constable, his first wife Lady Marianne and their furniture (I.H.) 85

Chapter Fifteen - Sir Clifford and his second wife Lady Rosina, an overlap of taste (I.H.) 88

Chapter Sixteen - Epilogue (I.H.) 92

(Initials in brackets indicate authorship of individual chapters)

PREFACE

During the months of January and February 1970 an Exhibition was mounted at the Ferens Art Gallery entitled "William Constable As Patron". This introduced us to an extraordinary man who lived during the majority of the 18th Century, in an isolated area of Britain, and who created a great monument to posterity in the form of one of the finest Houses and Collections in the country at that time, and he did all this with the restrictions which were imposed upon him as a Roman Catholic during that period.

Today we learn more about William Constable, and the text of this book is a lesson in bringing to life the career and achievements of a compassionate and intellectual man. All of us who read this script and see this Exhibition can bless him for such a wonderful experience, particularly in the knowledge and hope that for many generations to come his achievements will be enjoyed by many thousands of people.

This is a magnificent and detailed account of his life.

It is difficult to remember exactly when Burton Constable ceased to be a mass of bricks and mortar and chattels, and became a close friend, but for thirty years the inspiration which I gained through being involved in my own home is something I value as much as friendship.

I remember my grandfather once saying in 1938, when he was walking across from the house we were then living in to Burton Constable, that he believed his daily visits kept it alive. At that time there seemed little hope for a place which had been empty for 50% of the preceeding century.

However, government grants during the 60's and 70's saved the house, and from the early 1960's onwards one's faith was consolidated through the dedicated research of Dr. Ivan Hall and his wife, Elisabeth, and the subject matter of this book is a testament to their integrity and knowledge. There are others to whom we owe thanks, including Christopher Gilbert of Temple Newsam, John Bradshaw, Curator of Museums and Art Galleries, Kingston-upon-Hull, and the late Colonel Rupert Alec-Smith.

Thirty years of continued research and devotion to Burton Constable by Dr. Ivan Hall and his wife, Elisabeth, will, I hope, continue into the future and I believe that what we read today in this magnificent book will form the basis of a piece of vital historical fact which must be built on for future generations.

It remains for me to offer most sincere congratulations to the Halls, and particularly to Mr. Arthur Credland, Keeper of Maritime History, Hull City Museums and Art Galleries, in the preparation of this work. As the present incumbent of the Constable family, I can only remind myself that neither us nor Burton Constable would have survived in this way without the help of these people.

It is an honour to remain involved in this great monument to posterity.

John Chichester-Constable

FOREWORD

Hull City Museums and Art Gallery's last exhibition of material from Burton Constable at Ferens Art Gallery in 1970 was particularly devoted to the personality and patronage of William Constable, the Hall's great 18th century owner and connoisseur. Dr. Ivan Hall, then lecturing in the Adult Education Department of Hull University, with his wife, Elisabeth, had brought great enthusiasm to the study of both the archives and the surviving furnishings of the house, at a time when it had suffered much neglect. They were able to bring to light much information about William Constable's interests and acquisitions, particularly his patronage of local craftsmen and also the fruits of his travels and contacts with European personalities.

Their enthusiasm and the great efforts of Mr. John Chichester-Constable and his late wife, Gaye, enabled much more of the house to be renovated and made accessible to public visits. It remains a great house, of imposing proportions and fascinating contents, with a history of recusancy which helped to keep it isolated and unchanging. Its position, in Holderness to the east of Hull, still keeps it removed from much of the heritage tourism of today.

Dr. and Mrs. Hall have now left the Hull district but their studies and researches have continued, and their enthusiasm, if anything, has increased. In Arthur Credland, Hull's Keeper of Maritime History, they have found a collaborator who has been able to bring together more information about Hull merchants, tradesmen and craftsmen, particularly those associated with gunsmithing and the manufacturing of equipment for the whaling trade and its products. He has had further assistance from Michael J. Boyd, Hull's Assistant Keeper of Natural History, who has studied William Constable's collections of geological and zoological specimens.

A new exhibition, therefore, enables us to bring the account of research up to date, to include the range of artefacts and specimens on show and to include new information about the patronage of another generation, Sir Clifford Constable and his two wives.

We are pleased that this relationship between our city and such a great neighbouring house, and its present owner, continues to be strengthened. Its wealth and religious affiliation must have made it remote from our staunchly protestant forbears, although we begin to understand more of the effects of the Constable patronage and of the different levels of social life in the city and its region. Today we are trying to create new systems of patronage for arts and local industry. The study of great patrons in the past highlights the need. And we believe that the refurbishment of Burton Constable can be linked with the reconstruction of our city centre, after its years of industrialisation, destruction and neglect, to mutual benefit. This exhibition, with its accompanying book, published by Hutton Press, is a further step in proving that Hull and its region, has much history to offer both its residents and visitors, and that, once again, as Cobbett is quoted as writing in 1830, it is a place to 'look back to with delight'.

Trevor P. Larsen
Chairman, Cultural Services Committee

John Bradshaw
Curator of Museums & Art Galleries

ACKNOWLEDGEMENTS

Grateful thanks to all the people who have helped in the presentation of the material contained in this book, a process of research which has taken many years during which Mr. John Chichester-Constable has allowed us the freedom of his house and archive.

Generous grants came from the Royal Society, BP Chemicals (Easington) and Reckitt and Colman to undertake various projects and thanks are also due to:-

R.G.W. Anderson, C. Boddington, M.J. Boyd, D. Brydes, A.J. Clarke, E. Clarke, B. Cope, A.G. Credland, P. Davis, W.D. Hackmann, J. Hammond, K. Holt, S. Lane, F. Maddison, A. and J. Myers, J. Prescott, D. Rushman, A.E. Sandford, A. Simcock, C. Thompson,
G. L'E Turner, H. Walton, D. Webster and pupils of Beverley High and Beverley Grammar joint VIth form (1979-81).

The majority of photographs have been prepared for the booklet by Graham Edwards of the Hull City Museums.

Ivan and Elisabeth Hall,
August 1991.

INTRODUCTION

The following text aims to give an insight into the evolution of an outstanding country house during the eighteenth and nineteenth centuries. The Constables remained loyal to the 'old faith' and as Roman Catholics were debarred from seeking public office or even attending an English university. William Constable (1721-91) was educated at Douai and his early exposure to French culture was to prove a significant factor in the development of his taste and thought. The fact that as a Catholic he was unable to involve himself in the expense of becoming a member of parliament also meant that his fortune was available to be spent on the improvement of his estate and the beautification of his house. Proud of a long lineage he was always regretful of the loss of the family peerage with the death in 1718 of the fourth Viscount Dunbar without issue. Paradoxically William who was very much a man of the Age of Reason was greatly attached to the liberal and democratic ideas of Voltaire and Rousseau which were to help spark the French revolution shortly before his death. Constable briefly met Rousseau during the latter's visit to England in 1766 and had further contact with him in France in 1770 during his third Grand Tour. In a lively letter to his half brother Marmaduke Tunstall he describes their encounter:-

Lyons, May 15-16, 1770

Dear Duke!

This waits upon you from Lyons where I have been some days. We are all well, tho' somewhat fatigued on our arrival from rough roads and long journey, and bad lodgings, that is all except myself. We had common road adventures, broke an axle tree, which stopped us one day, and threw us into bad houses the rest of the journey, some hair-breath driving, some squabbles and all that. Come from Bruxelles, by Versailles, missed Paris and so by the Bourbonnois to Lyons - ushered into Lyons with a shower of snow on the 7th of May. Spring there more backward as to trees, hedges, corn, than is usual in Yorkshire. Visited Chantilly, saw a good cabinet of natural history. The hills in view of this town that separate Dauphiné from Savoy as much if not more covered with snow this 15th of May, than ever I saw our moors. Shall stay here a few days more to get Summer suits made for Italy, then for a fortnight to Geneva and then for trouts upon Mount Cenis. This a stupid manufacture town 180,000 inhabitants, of which 80,000 are paid for labour. I sacrificed some hours of rest, and boldly wrote a French letter to the best writer of the age (i.e Rousseau); however it answered my purpose, he appointed an hour and I attended. I laid aside all apprehension of language and conversed with him, with openness upon such subjects as come home to men. He seemed not displeased with my jargon, desired leave to wait upon me, which you may be sure, I did not refuse. His wife, a simple, plain nurse-like woman. He calls himself *Le plus paresseux des hommes*. Says he avoids company, from not knowing the ways and customs of worldlings and not being equal to their conversation. What a satire Dr. Duke! upon chit-chat![1]

The letter represented here only in excerpt demonstrates his lively and enquiring mind and includes reference to a number of his enthusiasms; he notes seeing a cabinet of natural history, mentions the continental method of yoking oxen as well as commenting on books of metaphysics and botany and the state of his health. Though always something of a hypochondriac Constable was latterly a martyr to gout.

The details of the reconstruction of Burton Constable and its furnishing by both William and Sir Clifford Constable are derived from the surviving vouchers and account books now preserved in the County Record Office in Beverley. Most of the work was executed by local men and the researches of Dr. Ivan and Elisabeth Hall are a revelation of the extraordinary range of skills and talent available in Hull, Beverley and York during the heyday of the house. Hull was a major European trading port throughout the whole of this period and became the centre of an extensive timber trade which provided the raw material for these carvers and furniture makers. The ease of contact with the continent provided many opportunities for the introduction of new ideas and fashions and the resident craftsmen were by no means deprived of external stimulation.

It is interesting that in 1812 Thomas Meggitt, whose workshop undertook a wide variety of tasks at Burton Constable including japanning, varnishing, repairing picture frames, gilding and even cleaning the garden statuary, advertised that:

'he stains and paints room, in the German fashion now so prevalent in London; and is in possession of patterns printed in Vienna to various designs for ceilings and walls together with a room furnished in his house done under the inspection of Mr. Barton of Vienna'.[2]

Mr. Barton was a certain William Barton (d. 1814), originally of Hull, who was a panorama painter and occasional marine artist. He went to live in Austria after touring Robert Barker's panorama of London and set up on his own account displaying panoramas of his own design in Vienna and around Europe.[3]

Hull was undoubtedly a much more cosmopolitan place in the eighteenth and nineteenth centuries than most of us can now imagine. In this respect it is interesting to have the glowing testimonial of William Cobbett, the radical reformer, who visited the city in 1830:

'It is a little city of London: streets, shops everything like it; clean as the best parts of London and the people are bustling and attentive. The town of Hull is surrounded with commodious docks for shipping. These docks are separated in three or four places by drawbridges so that as you walk round the town you walk by the side of the dock and the ships . . . . I hate commercial towns, in general: there is generally something loathsome in the look and so stern and unfeeling in the manners of sea-faring people that I have always, from my very youth disliked sea-ports but really the sight of this nice town, the manners of the people, the civil and kind and cordial reception that I met with, and the clean streets, and especially the pretty gardens in every direction, as you walk into the country have made Hull though a seaport a place that I shall always look back to with delight.'[4]

The building of the first enclosed dock, completed in 1778, opened up the city to development and with the completion of the Town Docks system in 1829 the enclosing medieval walls were finally laid low. Trade continued to expand throughout the nineteenth century, the Wilson Line sending its vessels to India and North America as well as Europe and the Mediterranean and the thriving whaling trade when it declined was replaced by the North Sea fishery.

The story of Hull and the great country house of Burton Constable are inextricably entwined and one hopes that further research will enable something more of the heady social life in Sir Clifford's time to be revealed. For example, Isabel Arundell the future Lady Burton was a kinsman of Sir Clifford and she records in the memoir of her husband Sir Richard Francis Burton, the explorer and arabist, how she was staying in the hall at Christmas 1860 when 'There was a large party in the house and we were singing, someone propped up the music with the *Times* which had just arrived, and the first announcement that caught my eye was that Capt. R.F. Burton had arrived from America'.[5]

Arthur G. Credland, Editor.
July 1991.

8

FAMILY TREE

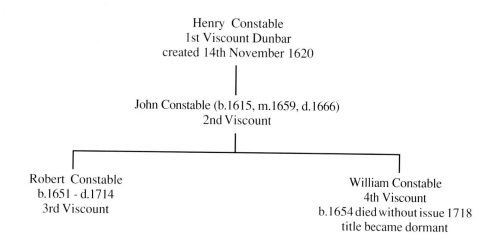

Henry Constable
1st Viscount Dunbar
created 14th November 1620

John Constable (b.1615, m.1659, d.1666)
2nd Viscount

Robert Constable
b.1651 - d.1714
3rd Viscount

William Constable
4th Viscount
b.1654 died without issue 1718
title became dormant

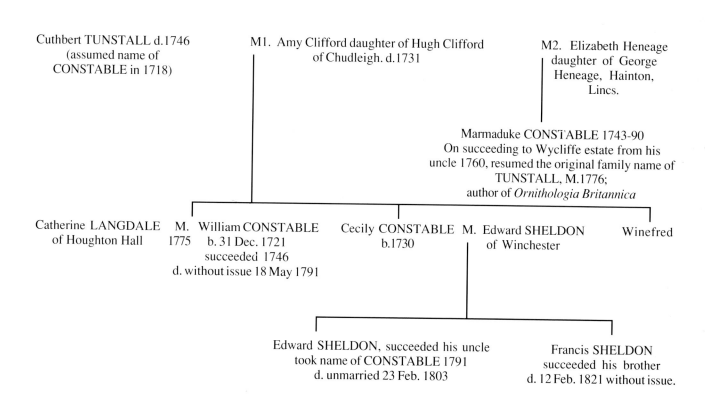

Cuthbert TUNSTALL d.1746
(assumed name of
CONSTABLE in 1718)

M1. Amy Clifford daughter of Hugh Clifford
of Chudleigh. d.1731

M2. Elizabeth Heneage
daughter of George
Heneage, Hainton,
Lincs.

Marmaduke CONSTABLE 1743-90
On succeeding to Wycliffe estate from his
uncle 1760, resumed the original family name of
TUNSTALL, M.1776;
author of *Ornithologia Britannica*

Catherine LANGDALE
of Houghton Hall

M.   William CONSTABLE
1775   b. 31 Dec. 1721
succeeded 1746
d. without issue 18 May 1791

Cecily CONSTABLE
b.1730

M. Edward SHELDON
of Winchester

Winefred

Edward SHELDON, succeeded his uncle
took name of CONSTABLE 1791
d. unmarried 23 Feb. 1803

Francis SHELDON
succeeded his brother
d. 12 Feb. 1821 without issue.

Francis CONSTABLE was succeeded by his cousin Thomas Hugh Clifford of Tixall, Staffs.,
grandson of Hugh, Baron Clifford, the father of Amy Clifford (wife of Cuthbert Constable)

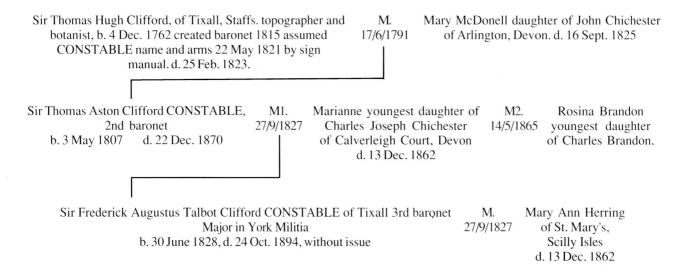

Sir Thomas Hugh Clifford, of Tixall, Staffs. topographer and   M.   Mary McDonell daughter of John Chichester
botanist, b. 4 Dec. 1762 created baronet 1815 assumed   17/6/1791   of Arlington, Devon. d. 16 Sept. 1825
CONSTABLE name and arms 22 May 1821 by sign
manual. d. 25 Feb. 1823.

Sir Thomas Aston Clifford CONSTABLE,   M1.   Marianne youngest daughter of   M2.   Rosina Brandon
2nd baronet   27/9/1827   Charles Joseph Chichester   14/5/1865   youngest daughter
b. 3 May 1807   d. 22 Dec. 1870   of Calverleigh Court, Devon   of Charles Brandon.
d. 13 Dec. 1862

Sir Frederick Augustus Talbot Clifford CONSTABLE of Tixall 3rd baronet   M.   Mary Ann Herring
Major in York Militia   27/9/1827   of St. Mary's,
b. 30 June 1828, d. 24 Oct. 1894, without issue   Scilly Isles
d. 13 Dec. 1862

The baronetcy became extinct with the death of Sir Frederick and he was succeeded by his cousin
Walter George Raleigh Chichester who assumed the additional name of Constable.
Walter was the grandson of Mary Barbara Constable and Colonel Sir Charles Chichester, youngest son of C. J. Chichester
of Calverleigh, Devon. The latter was also the grandfather of Sir Frederick.

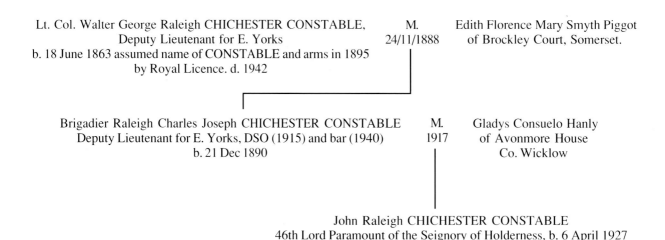

Lt. Col. Walter George Raleigh CHICHESTER CONSTABLE,   M.   Edith Florence Mary Smyth Piggot
Deputy Lieutenant for E. Yorks   24/11/1888   of Brockley Court, Somerset.
b. 18 June 1863 assumed name of CONSTABLE and arms in 1895
by Royal Licence. d. 1942

Brigadier Raleigh Charles Joseph CHICHESTER CONSTABLE   M.   Gladys Consuelo Hanly
Deputy Lieutenant for E. Yorks, DSO (1915) and bar (1940)   1917   of Avonmore House
b. 21 Dec 1890   Co. Wicklow

John Raleigh CHICHESTER CONSTABLE
46th Lord Paramount of the Seignory of Holderness, b. 6 April 1927

CHAPTER ONE

THE CONSTABLE INHERITANCE: 1718-1870

The death of Robert Constable, the last Viscount Dunbar in 1718 without a direct male heir was to be the first of a sequence of inheritances through the female line, often to branches of the family whose principal seat was elsewhere. On the other hand, new blood, and the amalgamation of estates, brought new ideas and created new opportunities from which Burton Constable has gained positive benefit. There is no doubt, however, that successive generations have regretted the family loss of title and, in varying degrees, found adherence to Roman Catholicism a handicap, if only because such adherence thrust them outside the mainstream of English social, political and educational life, and because the need to marry into families of co-religionists, restricted the choice of potential partnerships. The Jacobite rebellions of 1715 and 1745, and the Gordon Riots of 1780, can only have hindered the cause of Catholic Emancipation, though the laws restricting Catholic places of worship were modified in 1789, but emancipation did not arrive until 1829 and was not fully achieved for another forty years. Thus for the whole period under review, the Constables suffered some, though steadily diminishing, disability. Their private worship was held on the topmost floor of the south tower, a limited space that could hold only the family and their immediate servants. The Act that came into force in 1789 permitted public worship if it was discreetly conducted, and, in anticipation, William Constable commissioned from Thomas Atkinson of York a new chapel in nearby Marton.[6] This was spacious enough to contain tenants as well as servants, though to comply with the Act, the true function of the building had not to be readily recognisable.

More than forty years later, the Clifford Constables converted William Constable's coffee room cum billiard room into a handsome new chapel, whose altar fitted neatly into the east facing apse.[7] Now, for the first time, the Chapel became a part of the circuit of principal reception rooms. Because of changes such as these, Burton Constable represents an interesting, and therefore complex, microcosm of English taste, from the mid-Georgian to the High Victorian periods, but through a special combination of circumstances, additional factors were brought into play that are not normally present, and which were to diminish in importance from the middle of the nineteenth century onward.

The two most obvious of these special factors are the adherence to the Old Faith and the consequent social, political, and educational problems that followed.

Nonetheless they were there, and men of William Constable's generation had lived through the 'war' of 1745 and its anti-catholic rioting, centred on London, though not confined to it, of 1780. Constable will have seen the tall monument erected by a fellow Yorkshireman, Lord Rockingham, celebrating the defeat of the Young Pretender in the '45, and his own estate workers were anxiously to band together to defend Burton Constable during the weeks following the Gordon Riots of 1780. He was also acutely conscious not only of the 'loss' of the Viscountcy of Dunbar because of a failure of the male line after 1718, but also to the fact that Viscountcy was of the Kingdom of Scotland, not of England, and was a grant to an Englishman that precluded sitting in the English House of Lords.

The effective disbarment from English politics had interesting consequences. If the Constables were freed of the costly expenditure of fighting elections, money that they could therefore spend elsewhere, their effective lack of social and political power cut them off from English Court society and advancement, a factor that thrust them as 'dissidents' into the very different social circles of Catholic Europe. If little now seems recorded of William Constable's European contacts during his successive Grand Tours (c. 1741-2, c. 1764-5, and c. 1769-71), one is on surer ground with his earlier nineteenth successors.

Sir Thomas Constable had entertained the future Louis XVIII during his exile in England, while his son Sir Clifford, was a regular frequenter of the courts of Louis Philippe and Napoleon III. Unsurprisingly, French influences abound at Burton Constable throughout the period under review, but in William's day there was the secondary influence of neo-classicism with its emphasis on an improvement in manners, morals and taste, a seeking to return to a republican golden age uncorrupted by the excesses of the Roman Emperors that followed.

The refurbishment of Burton Constable owed most to two owners, William Constable (1721-1791) and Sir Clifford Constable (1807-1870). The first virtually rebuilt and refurnished the house, leaving only enough of his ancestral home to make clear his family's long lineage. During the thirty years that followed his death, the estate was maintained rather than developed by his two bachelor successors, Edward (17??-1803) and Francis (17??-1821) Sheldon (Constable), who successively adopted the Constable name and who inherited as descendants of William's sister Cecily.

Because neither Sheldon had heirs, the Constable estates passed to a Clifford branch of the family, this time descending through Amy, Cuthbert Constable's first wife.

Sir Thomas Clifford (1762-1823) also added the name Constable to his own when he took over the latter's estates in 1821, but his ownership was short-lived, for he died two years later, to be succeeded by his son, Thomas Aston Clifford Constable (1807-1870). The father had little opportunity to do much to Burton Constable, for his chief seat remained Tixall near Stafford, then recently rebuilt, and a house more conveniently situated for those who actively enjoyed London life. The elder Clifford had maintained far stronger links with France than the family at Burton Constable, but his entertainment of Louis XVIII did not, however, secure for the Cliffords the hoped-for peerage; George IV during his Regency, grudgingly granted a baronetcy in 1814.

The younger Clifford was too well aware that he had, by chance, inherited great wealth. It was claimed that in his day his combined estates totalled approximately 80,000 acres. What he failed to grasp was that his widely scattered estates required management of the highest order, not least during the agricultural booms and slumps that were to take place during his lifetime.

Instead he adopted a policy of extravagant pursuit of his own pleasures, irrespective of their effect upon his estates, which quickly became encumbered with a mountain of debt, a policy in which his son, Augustus Talbot, participated during his father's lifetime.

There followed a period of a quarter of a century of retrenchment (1870-1894) at Aston House in Ferriby the one time villa of William Wilberforce. In the interim, Burton Constable was stripped of its furniture and abandoned as a house. Sir Augustus (1828-1894) had no legitimate heirs and the estates passed to the Chichester branch of the family, who in 1894 found Burton Constable empty and neglected. It was empty because Sir Augustus' stepmother had exercised her right under the will of her husband, to take out of the house such items as she though necessary to support her position as the widow of a baronet. The will did, however, stipulate, that all such items were to be offered back to her late husband's successors should she no longer require them. Lady Rosina was to remarry twice, to Edward Trelawney, a marriage that ended in his death within a year, and to an Italian nobleman who outlived her. He is said to have accepted the terms under which his late wife had acquired the furniture from Burton Constable, but not that any offer of return must be free of charge. In the event, the Chichester-Constables paid for the furniture to be returned from Italy, and Burton Constable was restored once again to receive it.

This brief outline conceals a story of much greater complexity, for during Sir Clifford's lifetime, patronage was shared. Sir Clifford, acting through his trustees, was a 'tenant for life'. He had received the house and its 'heirloom' contents in good condition, and it was his duty so to maintain them. He could therefore justify expenditure to that end, but he was under no obligation to redecorate or refurbish in accordance with the latest fashions. His wife Marianne, or her sister Eliza Chichester (who also lived at Burton Constable), could spend their private fortunes on refurnishing or redecorating should they so wish, without the interference of the trustees. The sisters' expenditure is not easy to gauge, because it did not have to go through the estate's accounting system. Lady Marianne died in 1862 and her sister Eliza, apparently the same year. For some years before that, Sir Clifford had been unfaithful to his wife, but he did not marry his mistress, Rosina Brandon, until 1865. As far as is known, she did not enjoy a substantial personal fortune, a lack that did not curb her many extravagances. Her debts were thus added to those already burdening Sir Clifford's estates, and because of this, they became the basis of a case in the Court of Chancery, that was started in 1871 but was still unresolved in the early 1890's.[8] The case not only touched upon an immoral lifestyle; it brought to light dubious business practices on the part of almost all those firms who had received the patronage of Sir Clifford and Lady Rosina in the years following their marriage. The matter was further complicated by the couple's purchase and total refurbishing of a Thames-side villa at Teddington, which they renamed Dunbar House, after the late Viscount Dunbar, William Constable, who had died in 1718.

1. Oval portrait of William Constable (1721-91);
painted by Henry Walton.

2. *Anonymous painting of Burton Constable Hall in the seventeenth century before alterations by Cuthbert Constable and his successors.*

3. *Anonymous drawing of Burton Constable Hall, east front.*
Note the arms and supporters of the last Viscount Dunbar over the entrance.
(Map Room, British Library)

CHAPTER TWO

ARCHITECTURAL DEVELOPMENT OF BURTON CONSTABLE

The house at Burton Constable grew piecemeal. It's earliest component is the north tower, a massively vaulted structure of brick and stone, its purpose much like that of the other tower houses of Holderness, a building capable of being defended against the casual raiders who harassed the coastal strip where the Humber joins the North Sea.[9] The rest of the house, and those once adjoining, would be of a lightweight timber framework that could not readily by protected against fire or violence. The Constable's principal seat before the Elizabethan era was at Halsham, and because this was said to be even more liable to attack, the decision was made c.1570 to utilise the tower at Burton Constable, add a one-room deep wing southwards, and complete the new range by a second tower approximately similar to the first. Such a layout had much earlier parallels in the area, for example, Wressle Castle of c.1380 or the later, c.1585, Howley Hall near Leeds. Next came two externally symmetrical wings projecting from the eastern faces of the two towers - the southern one containing the great kitchen and new domestic offices; the northern one, the sets of lodging rooms, disposed collegiate fashion. At the centre of the east front, there was a huge oriel window lighting the Great Hall, the latter approached by a modest doorway that opened into the screens passage. The chief features on the then west front were the polygonal staircase turrets whose ogee domes rose well above parapet level. The southern one retains its spiral stairs intact, but the base of its northern counterpart was transformed into a vestry for the priest once the billiard room had been converted into a chapel.[10]

The exterior was completed by an outer and an inner courtyard, the latter given greater consequence by a centrally placed gatehouse such as survives at nearby Burton Agnes, and round the outside of the southern and eastern courtyard walls ran the public highroad from Hull and Sproatley to Marton. The two-storeyed stable block

was discreetly sited north eastward of the north tower, its crowstepped gables in marked contrast to the remainder.[11]

The Elizabethan main house, with its Jacobean wings, was essentially symmetrical, but after the Civil War, new rooms were added to extend the south front, first westward, the first component of the Gallery range, and southward, the Stucco room. The larger extension at first retained the mullioned windows in the older style, but the latter was equipped with sash windows in the newer taste, an ambivalence of style was to be continued during succeeding ownerships.

Thus the decision to double the depth of the main range by adding a suite of rooms parallel to it to serve as a new west front was initiated by Cuthbert Constable (alias Cuthbert Tunstall) (16??-1746) and completed by his son William (1721-1791).

Georgian Improvements

The first put two ranges of modern sash windows in between his mullioned centrepiece and the earlier south-western corner, a pattern continued by his son from the 1750's to the 1770's. Hence in his duplication of the south-western corner pavilion at the north-western angle, there are mullioned windows facing west, but blind sash windows on the north or return front.[12]

This compromise was visually unsatisfactory and, during the ownership of Sir Clifford Constable (b.1807 - d.1870), the sashes were removed throughout the west front, though left on the north and south fronts.

At the same time, Sir Clifford tried to ameliorate another Georgian 'improvement', William Constable had redirected the principal approach from the great south avenue to one that was considered more picturesque. This new drive was first to pass through 'Capability' Brown's enclosing shelter belt, then cross the new bridge that divided the upper and lower lakes, a bridge sited so as to give a distant oblique view of the southern and western fronts. Seen across the water from such a vantage point, this distant view of Burton Constable recalled golden stone houses such as Burghley, but to heighten that comparison, the red East Yorkshire brick had to be coated with an Italian yellow ochre, and it was this ochre that Sir Clifford ordered painstakingly to be removed.

Similar decisions had had to be taken by William Constable as regards the gardens and the park. A plan of 1755 showed how strips of the medieval open field system and the straight avenues of the Baroque period came almost up to the house. There were, however, urns, paths, flowers and fruit trees within the two walled enclosures on the eastern front. If 'improvements' were to be made here, the walled enclosures would have to go, as would the avenues that radiated from the house.[13]

For virtually the decade following Cuthbert Constable's death, his son toyed with numerous ideas which were then put to his chosen advisers - 'Capability' Brown, John Carr of York, Thomas Atkinson of York, Timothy Lightoler and Robert Adam. Brown, Carr, and Lightoler all submitted far reaching schemes, while Atkinson probably, and Adam definitely, were only consulted about internal redecoration. Lightoler almost certainly made sure that his own fees were notably less than those of his rivals, and with a steady tongue and a readier drawing pen, he quickly guaged his client's ever changing stylistic requirements. Lightoler's total charge for drawings and 'attendance' came to £63 (many of Lightoler's drawings remain in the collection) while Adam had charged £18 for the interior of a single room, i.e. one laid out drawing for the four walls and a separate sheet for the ceiling.[14]

Lightoler was as adept as any nineteenth century architect in producing schemes in any style: Gothick, Jacobethan, Rococo, Palladian and neo-classical, were all paraded for his patron's inspection, some as pencil sketches, others in full colour. Lightoler's assiduity and eclecticism paid full dividends, and it is to him more than anyone else that Burton Constable owes its present form

and appearance. This needs only the qualification that William Constable remained the arbiter of taste. It was he who decided to destroy the great Elizabethan hall screen and to set aside Carr's nobler scheme for the Great Hall in favour of Lightoler's far weaker design,[15] and in his placing the huge range of glasshouses on the west lawn adjacent to his new west front, he showed a lack of understanding of the underlying principles of landscape gardening, a decision he soon regretted and expensively rectified.[16] Not until the late 1770's did Constable simply accede to the fashionable - here represented by the Great Drawing Room by James Wyatt, with its splendidly carved chimneypiece by John Bacon and its complete furnishing by the two Thomas Chippendales. Even here the ever generous Constable had offered a final chance to Thomas Atkinson, possible a co-religionist and certainly a Yorkshireman deserving encouragement and one whom he continued to employ. These late designs were for the Coffee Room, the present Blue Drawing Room in the centre of the west front, the new 'Dry House' or Orangery and the new Marton Roman Catholic Chapel, as well as smaller commissions for marble chimneypieces. Shortly after William Constable's death, his successor Edward Sheldon (Constable) commissioned Atkinson to design the family mausoleum near the former family seat at Halsham.[17]

4. *Sarcophagus with carved gilt Bacchic tiger by Jeremiah Hargrave; one of a pair of such caskets to hold unfinished wine bottles.*

5. *Table by John Lowry of Hull and London with scagliola top by Domenico Bartoli, featuring a central motif of Britannia.*

CHAPTER THREE

WILLIAM CONSTABLE - HIS IDEAS AND IDEALS

William Constable could serve as a model for a man of the Enlightenment, a movement with a philosophical approach to life that brought together men as different as Voltaire and Rousseau and that profoundly influenced the despotic regimes of Frederick the Great, Maria Therese and Catherine the Great.

The Enlightenment, with its stress upon Reason, upon Liberty, as clearly encouraged modern science as it discouraged religious superstition. In art there was an attempt to revive the styles of Ancient Greece and Republican Rome, with their clean forms and refined detail, while in gardening there was much emphasis upon the freedom and naturalness of the Landscape Garden. If Constable was rebuffed by Voltaire, he was host to, and received by Rousseau. Inevitably the adoption of the ideas and ideals of the Enlightenment brought with it many conflicts. For example to create a Landscape Garden meant the sacrifice of the great Avenues planted by ones ancestors - always a difficult choice and one on which Constable hesitated. He was almost certainly a Deist, yet he immediately provided a Roman Catholic chapel at Marton as soon as the law permitted it, while he consistently treated all he employed as men and women whom he trusted and who in their turn were promptly and fully paid. His own immediate employees were not only encouraged toward prosperity, but when occasion arose, treated to visits to the theatre when able and to pensions when retired.

As a man of the Enlightenment, Constable was clearly of the eighteenth century, but one can also sense that he was in other respects what might be called a proto-Victorian. His honesty as to his Mass going lost him his first love, Ann, daughter of Viscount Fairfax, who in her turn never married, while Constable did not marry his subsequent love until after the death of his own much loved sister Winefred. By that time he was fifty four and his bride beyond the reasonable age of child bearing.

Ultimately the hall and its embellishment was the great focus of a life filled with a wide variety of interests and intellectual pursuits.

William Constable found himself in an interesting situation symbolised by his election to both the Society of Antiquaries and to the Royal Society. Unlike many members of the Society of Antiquaries, he did not seek to preserve either his own Tudor mansion or its furniture for their own sake - and here he differed from his near neighbour, Sir Griffith Boynton of Burton Agnes, who modified that house to make it more convenient but without the wholesale destruction of the interior that took place at Burton Constable. On the other hand, in the medieval way, Constable regarded his three dozen or so immediate servants as his *family*, and from time to time dined with them off simple fare in the Great Hall. No doubt also because they were his *family*, he ensured that they were well and promptly paid, the more so when they worked overtime, and, even when one abandoned him, making sure that the person was paid a half pension.[18] Unlike most fellow Georgian gentlemen, he protested when a supplier was tardy in rendering an account: he wrote to one of them 'it is not my custom to owe for so long'.[19] On the other hand, he was excessively proud of his lineage and went to unusual lengths to display it, in the full knowledge of those Roman writings deploring such vanity. Constable, for example, ordered for the exterior of the house, a display of the arms, supporters and coronet of his grandfather, the last Viscount Dunbar, (d.1718) forty years after his death, while indoors the visitor was greeted with a display of family heraldry within the cove of the ceiling - some 28 coats in all, plus a shield with 35 quarterings in Bartoli's scagliola over the chimneypiece, as well as numerous chairs and table frames also bearing the Constable's arms or dragon crest. For those not aware of the Constable family's alliances, a guide book was made available, and several richly illuminated genealogical family trees were mounted on rollers for those with the leisure and interest to study them. He even went so far as to commision fake portraits of more recent ancestors to create a full sequence from Sir Henry Constable to his own day. Those original portraits that were merely a head and shoulders he had extended with arms, legs, and an appropriate background. In his notebooks, however, he transcribed fragments such as those from Martial or Juvenal, indicating his full awareness of what he was doing.

Constable's remodelling of Burton Constable between 1755 and 1785 created a house with sequences of huge rooms, mostly with good joinery and marble chimneypieces, but not otherwise richly decorated. The plainer rooms were thus dependant upon the colour and the pattern of the wallpaper, carpets, curtains, and furniture that complemented them. The obvious exceptions were the Great Hall, the Dining Room and the Great Drawing Room. The long term advantages proved to be that against such simple backgrounds it was possible to display furnishings of very different periods and styles without overt incongruity. That this is so is demonstrated by the fact that only the Dining and the Great Drawing Rooms have kept their original furniture essentially unchanged.

NEOCLASSICISM - decoration of the Dining Room

If his love of Antiquity was not enough to preserve his house, it did encourage him to study the current excavations at Pompeii and Herculaneum, particularly on his tour of 1764-5, and to translate many of the motifs he had seen there into decorative elements for his new furniture and fittings. His personal experience was supplemented by the study or purchase of books of engravings, of the latest archaeological discoveries, and of the many new volumes issued by G.B. Piranesi.[20] The latter sought the financial help of the Grand Tourists, and most of those to whom Piranesi dedicated his plates were not only British, but Catholic. His dedications included the names of William Constable and his sister Winefred.[21]

From such sources Constable gained an insight into Roman domestic architecture not available to earlier generations, and he returned to Burton Constable determined no longer to accept the still current Anglo-Palladian-Rococo, but to demand something more nearly Roman in order to transform his house from 'a bad old house without - into a good one within'. He was, however, constrained not only by the spatial volumes of the existing rooms, but by a curious reticence in his employment of architects. Like many contemporary Yorkshiremen, for example Sir Christopher Sykes of Sledmere, he sought value for money by approaching one architect after another in an attempt to achieve his ideal at the least cost.[22] One may suspect that to save money, he would see an architect in London, furnish him with the physical dimensions and the present appearance of the room, and then await their response. Robert Adam, for example, designed a new interior for the Dining Room and then sent Constable his account. The latter commented on the reverse of the ceiling design 'I paid him 18 guineas for this'. The 'mosaic' ceiling was one of Adam's favourites and, typical of the architect, the endmost octagons and intervening adjacent squares were left incomplete at the ceiling edges - an aesthetic device intended to increase the apparent size of the room. That Constable evidently objected is revealed by Timothy Lightoler's subsequent paraphrase, in which all the octagons are completed. This design, like the Rococo one that had preceded it, was rejected in favour of one much more closely modelled on an Antique painting. The outsized cameo above the chimneypiece directly reproduces an antique gem then in the possession of Baron Stosch - one of a collection later offered to William Constable with a view to purchase. The remaining stucco plaques are 'classical' but not strictly Antique, though the plaster figure of Bacchus is derived from one of the Pomfret marbles now in the Ashmolean Museum, Oxford.

Neither the overall proportions of the room nor its green, white and gold colour scheme, have been combined to suggest a truly Roman interior based upon colours such as black, terracotta, and yellow ochre, but if the room is not wholly neo-classical, no other contemporary Dining Room achieved a more convincing result. What is certain is that the interior, after his interventions, does represent Constable's personal taste.

Symbolism in the Dining Room

More schemes were prepared for the Dining Room than any other - first a Gothick design by Lightoler,[23] then one wholly Rococo. Next Adam and Atkinson submitted schemes, only to be rejected in turn. Finally Lightoler was asked first to re-work Adam's ceiling and then to devise something more positively in line with his patron's more highly developed neo-classical taste.

Unlike the earlier neo-classicism of Lord Burlington and William Kent, which was founded upon the architecture of ancient Roman temples and that of Andrea Palladio (1505-1580), this second wave of neo-classicism was based rather upon the newly discovered domestic work of the Roman era, albeit much of that knowledge was derived from wall and ceiling paintings, sculpture and mosaics. Given his independence of spirit, he might have achieved the first neo-Roman domestic interior. Instead, just as Chippendale advised, he chose a 'Variety of Hints sufficient to construct a new one', some Antique and some French, grafted onto an English stock, and generally to an English colour scheme. The ceiling is a simplification of one excavated at Gragnano near Stabia in 1759, i.e. the original very varied central motifs were here reduced to alternative whorls of acanthus, and in white and gold instead of polychrome.[24] The overall theme is an allusion to Bacchus, God of wine and hospitality. He presides over the side table, he rides the Bacchic tiger with Ariadne, a direct if greatly enlarged copy of a Graeco-Roman gem. The same tiger crouches on the two sarcophagi - pieces of mobile furniture used to hold partly finished bottles of wine should they be needed in another room. Tigers' heads also appear at regular intervals in the cornice and as parts of the principal doorheads, together with the vine trails her and elsewhere on the walls. The Bacchic theme is summed up in the great oval cameo wall plaque in which Bacchantes dance to a Satyr's pipes and infants discover the potency

of wine. There is, however, a second theme, that of fertility and birth. In Greek mythology Bacchus' own birth had been saved by the intervention of ivy leaves and these garland the two side tables. No less discreetly, a young but naked couple converse beneath a tree, their very youth in contrast to the elderly lonely figure perched near the upper corner of the plaque, whilst below him a goat suckles her young. That love is a gamble is depicted by Cheeres plaster sculpture group of Mercury watching over young Eros who is throwing the dice. All this activity would be impossible without health, here shown as Aesculapius, the god of medicine, to whom Hygeia offers a sacrifice attended by a hooded initiate, the last and final allusion to the fertility rites of Bacchus.

In one of Constable's notebooks there are references to drunkeness in the writings of 'Hippocrates, Dioscorides, Avicenna who think it conducive to health to Drink Wine Sometimes to Excess',[25] while 'Cato's Enemies could reproach him with no fault but Sometimes in Company (& that Seldom) with his friends, he would Indulge too freely in Wine'.[26]

On his third Grand Tour of 1769-1771, Constable had himself depicted as Cato in his portrait by Anton Maron.

This personal fusion of arts and sciences is likewise demonstrated by the design of a chimneypiece in the Kings Suite on the first floor where it is the sole ornament. The overall design was provided by Lightoler, who indicated Tower of the Winds type capitals for the columns, which were to be spirally garlanded in a celebratory mood. The capitals as executed were an amalgam of the Ancient and Modern Ionic, i.e. with angle volutes ornamented with a spiral of delicate ornament. Except for the spirals of oak leaves and ribbons, the design is conventional for its day. It is the side tablets that catch the eye, each with its undulating snake in the manner of a Pompeiian painting, but here each reptile is a rattlesnake of North American, not Roman, origin, a carefully calculated fusion of two branches of modern knowledge - the fauna of America and the excavations at Pompeii.[27] Constable went further in one of his notebooks: he says that a 'snake is a symbol of sensuality', and thus appropriate for a bedroom. Unfortunately the

6. *(left). Left side of the gun by Simpson of York which belonged to William Constable; this features the Britannia motif in inlaid silver wire. (The Board of Trustees of the Royal Armouries).*

7. *(below). An inlaid writing table by Thomas Walker, the handles are of carved mahogany glued to a wrought iron base, but maintaining the form of the typical brass handles of the day.*

inscription on the altar on the centre tablet is now indistinct and its symbolism obscure, e.g. to whom or by whom is the sacrifice offered. The altar is set into a mixed trophy of Roman military standards, a Bacchic wand, Mercury's caduceus, a hunting horn and Pan's double pipes. The end blockings have further Antique musical instruments - the lyre, cymbals, a Satyr's pipe and two horns, where Lightoler had suggested mere paterae. Unlike most of its type, the ornament is of brightly coloured scagliola inlaid into the white marble.(pl.2)

The nearby chimneypiece in the Long Gallery was carved by Thomas Issott of Beverley and has Tuscan pilasters overlaid with black scagliola, against a background of yellow Siena. Each pilaster is inlaid with a charming flower arrangement where a tall stake is driven into a clay plantpot. The stake, simulating a thorn branch, is wound round with a spiralling chain of garden flowers - some, like the lily of the valley, hollies or convolvulus, natives; others, such as the anemone japonica or tulip, exotics from the Far and Near East. Both pilasters have the same groupings but 'handed', and must surely represent the type of short-lived flower arrangement then deployed on special occasions.

The five tablets in the frieze are wholly different. At the centre is a ruin piece of the sort found on Florentine *pietra dura* of the day, though such ruins were also included as minor panels in Pompeiian and Herculaneum wall paintings. The same also holds for the pairs of side and end panels - the former, luscious garlands of plums, cherries, pears and grapes; the latter, exotic birds perched on twigs of plum.

Such a fusion of the wholly contemporary and the Antique is paralleled by the two scagliola tops made by Domenico Bartoli for John Lowry's 'Gallery tables'. The earlier one is signed by Bartoli, who worked in the house for 50 guineas per year from 1763 to 1765 and continued intermittently till 1766. It depicts victorious Britannia reclining upon a lion, surrounded by the fruits, flowers, weeds and foliage selected by Constable. The oak sprays symbolise unyielding strength and with Britannia, are clearly a tribute to British success in the Seven Year War (1756-1763). This centrepiece is framed by a ribbon of porphyry intertwined with convolvulus. The outer border has corner and centrepieces like the fashionable Italian picture frame with, in the centre, cartouches filled with fruit, symbols of Peace. The four cornerpieces recall a quite different theme - the Crusades - in which an earlier generation of the Constable family had played their part in a war between Christian and Infidel. The paraphernalia of war are here of classical, not medieval, design, but in the background stands a tall palm tree, whilst a captured standard displays the Crescent of Islam. If a Catholic can justly celebrate a modern British triumph, he can also remind himself of the Christian struggle in times when Catholics were freer.

The overall design is wholly Italianate such as had then been current for half a century, whilst its counterpart is as neo-classical.

Here again, the centre is a ruin piece complete with the Constable's motto and arms, but now set within a neo-classical mosaic of interlocking circles in gold, enclosing plaques of blue lapis lazuli and pink rosettes. The outer border, in part enclosed by a band of guilloche, has sprays of oak loosely scattered over the black surface.

This alternating mixture of the free and the geometric is mosaic-like, though without any obvious Antique source. It does, however, harmonise with the Doric legged table frame which supports is, for here too is a neo-classical treatment without a direct Antique parallel. If one compares these Gallery table frames with the designs in the newly published pattern books, one can see just how far advanced was William Constable's taste, and why, when his London agent, John Dunn, failed to interest London makers in Constable's ideas, the latter turned to local men who would 'hearken to his wishes . . . .'

The earliest of Constable's Doric table frames were probably those with the porphyry scagliola tops. Each column bears a square slice of entablature, but these are independent of each other, connected only by a hidden St. Andrew's cross of a strip of wrought iron as a support to the slab. Such an arrangement is, however, unstable, a defect remedied for the next pair which have their compressed entablatures linked by the usual wooden frame which is here inlaid with octagons, the larger ones inset with stylised four or six-petalled flowers. In the centre of the front rail is an inlaid tablet bearing the Constable's arms.

The use of inlaid woods had been frequent in the earlier decades of the century, but had declined with the advent of the Rococo when carved wood was favoured. This return to inlaid work coincided with the new fasion for small scale neo-classical detail, which was as easily inlaid as carved, but which had the additional virtue of novelty. Thus the work at Burton Constable is an early example of the revival of inlay. The use of inlay had never fallen out of fashion in France, and Constable was probably aware of this.

As elsewhere in his patronage, there is a positive linkage between items, inlaid scagliola for both table tops and chimneypiece, and a similar congruence between the columns of one and the pilasters of the other, while the Doric entablature also appears as the crowning element of the taller bookcases. In turn, these have inlaid stars in their metopes, a device repeated on the backs of the walnut chairs attributed to Wrightson of Beverley. One may go further. The decoration on William Constable's finest sporting gun is stylistically related to the Brittannia·table top.

The gun is not earlier than 1738, when William Simpson became a freeman of York, but the rococo style of ornament would be early for that date. Incorporated within the scrolls of the side plate is the dragon crest of the Constables. The stock is inlaid with silver wire inset with figures of Fame, Brittania, Mercury and a lion and unicorn, beneath a palm tree, all in a style closely similar to Bartoli's scagliola work of the early 1760's. It thus accords with William Constable's policy of linking together quite different articles through their decoration. Such an approach would have been uncommon in Cuthbert Constable's day, but not in the greater sophistication of his son's.

CHAPTER FOUR

THE CABINET OF SCIENTIFIC INSTRUMENTS

The surviving documentation shows that William Constable's cabinet of natural philosophy was mainly assembled after 1757. Two decades earlier, Constable's education at the Catholic school of Douai in northern France was significant in developing this special interest in science. In 1738 he entered the class 'Philosophy' which was intended for English students barred from studying in the universities in their own country, but who did not wish to take up Holy Orders. In the second year 'natural philosophy' was taken, and its curriculum included experimental work. Constable's chief aide in collecting was his London agent, the catholic priest John Dunn (1718-98) who had been similarly educated at Douai.[29]

In 1742 Constable completed his early education by touring France with his tutor 'Mr. Molyneux'[30] with whom he presumably went on botanical forays in and around Paris where he also observed the latest scientific experiments. In 1761 he wrote to his stepmother, persuading her to send her son, Marmaduke Tunstall, 'studying his second year Philosophy' to Paris rather than keep him on at school, for at Douai 'the second year is chiefly experimental and the Experiments are infinitely better performed at Paris than at Douai'. He goes on to say 'He might during the progress of the year see all the best cabinets relating to the study of natural philosophy'.[31] How Constable's own experience in Paris might have influenced his subsequent life as a scientist is revealed in a letter written in 1769 requesting a reference from the scientist, John Needham, to assist in obtaining an interview with Voltaire - he writes 'I am likewise a Collector, a bit of a Vertu, was once in esteem as an Electrician, am sometimes an Astronomer and have knowledge Enough of Natural History to distinguish your points . . .'[32]

The great sequence of purchases that can be traced from 1757 onward serve to reflect something of his scientific development. They also show how eagerly the instrument makers adapted their output not only to the new advances in the various branches of science and agriculture but also to the demands of gentlemen, keen to furnish their cabinets with fashionable demonstration models. Such a range of interests is shown in the influential book - *A Course on Experimental Philosophy* - by J.T. Desaguliers, whose second volume, published in 1745, was in the library at Burton Constable. Similar interests could have been found in other contemporary English cabinets such as that of the 3rd Earl of Bute, (1713-92), or in the surviving cabinet of the 3rd Earl of Egremont and his mistress at Petworth.[33] The same may be said of the large instrument collection of the 'professional' scientist Joseph Priestley. The pattern was also followed in the 'portable laboratories' of the itinerant lecturers in natural philosophy that taught in the larger provincial towns of England. Such men were following in public in the footsteps of Desaguliers, Francis Hauksbee, William Whiston as were the many Dissenters who likewise gave practical demonstrations in London on the New Philosophy and the New Chemistry during the 18th century. The influence of such cabinets demonstrated the popularisation and practice of science and has been discussed elsewhere.[36] The former group included Constable's demonstrator, John Arden (1721-91) the much travelled 'lecturer in experimental philosophy'.

It is known that Constable had come under Arden's influence by 1757 for he was engaged to give a private demonstration of static electricity experiments in December of that year and subsequently supplied chemicals, apparatus and pharmaceuticals to his patron. Arden, had just settled in Beverley and found it necessary to purchase his freedom in 1758. However he continued to travel, his lecture venues including Birmingham, Manchester and Liverpool. In the 1770's he set up a lecture room at 'his house' in St. James Street, Bath, the scientific apparatus being 'elegantly finished with the latest improvements'. Both Priestley and Arden were members of the Bath Philosophical Society founded in 1779, but the latter had also come into contact with Priestley at the Warrington Academy.[37]

Fortuitously Arden's lecture syllabus was published: *A short account of a course of Natural and Experimental Philosophy* by J. Arden Teacher of Experimental Philosophy at Bath. (Beverley, 1772).[38] It is notable that Constable's collection can be studied within the framework of topics covered in Arden's 12 lectures listed as follows: the general principles of the subject, attraction and repulsion, electricty (two), gravitation, mechanical powers, models illustrating a variety of mechanical and agricultural inventions, magnetism, the use of the globes, astronomy, hydrostatics, air, expansion of metals by heat, optics - illustrated by the use of microscopes and telescopes. This course was further elaborated in a booklet by Arden's son, James who had prepared it because his father was 'too much engaged in business'. Even though there have been some losses from the Constable collection nearly all Arden's course could still be given using the surviving items.

After the death of Constable's brother, Marmaduke in 1790, the former suggested a position for Arden near Wycliffe - 'Mr. Arden -might be employed Perhaps if not too Old for a year or Two, in Ovington or Girlington.[39] However Arden died in Beverley the following year having founded a notable family in the town.

Electrical instruments from Yorkshire and London

Constable's first documented purchases seem to justify the self styled epithet 'esteemed electrician'.[40] Among the many accounts concerning purchase and maintenance of electrical apparatus from the Hull whitesmith, Timothy Marshall and Beverley whitesmith, John Marshall this highly specialised equipment is listed alongside household and garden items.[41] One charge, 'A Brass Conductor by Mr. Arden £1.6.0.' could mean that either Marshall acted as middle man for Arden, which seems unlikely or that Arden designed the instrument to be manufactured by Marshall. Either way the instrument maker expanded the range of his technical skills. In January 1758 John Marshall charged £12.0.0 for 'A masheen for electricity with 2 Cushons 2 Chives 2 Combs & 2 Conductors'. Timothy Marshall's December 1758 account reveals that an 'Electric Cushing' is made of 7lbs of brass costing £9.4., covered with buckskin costing 0.15.0 and a 'padd' for 0.3.6. Clearly the two Marshall's were working in parallel for Constable.

Much of the above equipment has been identified by Hackmann as 'the remains of a Wilson type machine', - a design first published in 1750.[42] In December 1758 Arden wrote to a Mr. Charles Lawton, about the unexpectedly explosive results of his demonstration at Burton Constable in December 1757.[43] Was this a trial of the new equipment? Constable's own comments upon his experiments typically do not survive though copied notes of his and other's experiments occur in his notebooks. Arden also described an electric orrery that he had invented and had had made up by a whitesmith - perhaps one of the Marshalls. The use of non specialised local craftsmen by other early practitioners has been noted elsewhere.[44] Simultaneously Constable was ordering instruments, from the royal instrument maker Benjamin Cole Jnr. (1727-1813), including further electrical apparatus. In the following years equipment also came from another royal instrument maker George Adams (1704-73), but of this order less survives.[45]

Both Cole and Adams provided electrical machines in 1757 and 1767 respectively[46] but the accounts lack detail and therefore cannot be linked to the beautifully made single glass plate machine with Leyden jar and stand which Hackmann dates to the late 1760's. The painted wooden framed two plate machine and kit for which the brass handled carrying box has been found, similarly lacks a definite provenance: Nairne and Blunt repaired this machine in 1784. After 1774 this firm supplied the signed globe friction machine. Nairne's instructions for this machine describe associated apparatus, which is still extant, for example a signed 'Henley' electrometer.[47]

8. Condensing engine; within the two joined brass hemispheres a high pressure can be achieved and the compressed air tapped off for various experiments and demonstrations. Supplied by Benjamin Cole 1757. Height 20 inches, diameter 12 inches.

9. Model of the pile driver (height 15 inches), designed by Valoué, used in building Westminster Bridge (1735-7).

Astronomy and Optics

Constable's other self-styled 'profession' that of "astronomer" also resulted in annotations and accounts. His first recorded purchase was from a local craftsman, Robert Waddington (fl.1747-78) of Hull who sent, among other purchases, a Hadley's quadrant costing £2. According to E.G.R. Taylor - *Mathematical Practitioners of Hanoverian England* a Robert Waddington settled in Court Mills Lane, London in 1763, where he specialised in making an improved version of Hadley's quadrant - costing £4.7. He had taught at Portsmouth Academy but later he sold instruments to the Royal Society. He would not be the only craftsmen who had been helped on his way by Constable's early patronage.[48] However in 1758 Constable turned to London makers, buying the first of three achromatic telescopes from George Adams for £2.12.2 in the same year that Peter Dollond had received the Copley Metal for inventing achromatic lenses.[49] Constable bought a Dollond telescope in 1773 at the same time as the equatorial telescope from Henry Hindley (1701-71) of York which cost the very high figure of £105.[50] The sole survivors of this group are a portable telescope signed by Jesse Ramsden, a pocket telescope and a brass and mahogany telescope body.

An indication that Constable may have been interested in older and more ephemeral equipment, was the discovery among the apparatus on Landing 14, that is the top storey at Burton Constable, of an early 18th century cardboard volvelle and an astronomical chart signed by the cartographer Philip Lea (fl.1683-1700). The latter is on card and board with annotations for the year 1738 'from Leadbetter'.[51] There is also the much rarer ephemeral item, a card and board quadrant signed by Joseph Moxon (1627-1702). These items may have however have belonged to Constable's father, Cuthbert who was also an eminent natural philosopher.

Recording and drawing

Constable bought several microscopes but the only surviving microscopic equipment is a new construction first illustrated by George Adams in *Micrographia Illustrata* 1771.[53] It is the housing for an early and unusual version of a solar (or projection) microscope whose micrometer scale enables the reflecting mirror to be adjusted according to latitude. Though the pyramidal camera obscura connected to the above apparatus has not been traced there survives Cole's documented and signed large book camera obscura, which despite its cumbersome size is described as 'portable' (One should remember that Constable was not short of sturdy servants!). The camera obscura was operated on the principles described in Robert Smith's *Optics*.[54] It is closely similar to the one said to have belonged to Sir Joshua Reynolds and now displayed in the Science Museum, London, but the Burton Constable example has the additional refinements of a revolving lens and mirror housing. It was bought from Cole in 1757, costing together with a perspective view of Venice and its packing a total of £5.10.3.[55]

The instrument may also have also been used by Constable's sister, Winefred who was also fond of drawing. John Arden listed an intriguing use for the camera obscura:- 'Phosphori and other Bodies producing fire by Friction shewn in the Camera Obscura'[56] Constable's not unexpected interest in a type of instrument enabling him to fuse art with science, is also seen in the acquisition of a portrait camera obscura, recently identified as one of the few remaining 'Royal Delineators' made by Edward Storer of Lisle Street, London;[57] the latter was patented in 1778 and Constable subscribed to the author's 'Syllabus'. The lens system had been devised to give a particularly bright and clear image for the tracing of portraits, or other close up subjects perhaps in the Constable's case of plant specimens. Yet another London instrument maker, John Bennett, supplied a handsome brass and ivory signed pantograph in 1769, used to enlarge or diminish drawings or maps, an instrument here associated with Constable's favoured architect, Timothy Lightoler. Also signed are the two way-wisers by Thomas Heath (fl.1714-65) and George Adams.[58]

Pneumatics

Sixteen instruments have been identified out of Constable's generous orders from Benjamin Cole. Four of them are signed by the maker and many are concerned with pneumatics. In February 1757 Constable bought a Cole air pump 'with all ye neat apparatus' for 21 pounds, - the elegant Doric columned instrument was designed to harmonise with the Gallery at Burton Constable. It seems very likely that the still existing vacuum jars, imploding bottles and other types of pressure vessels are part of this 'neat apparatus'. Later in the year Constable was also to buy the guinea and feather apparatus and a double transferer for use with the air pump. In October the remarkable 'brass and glass condensing engine' arrived from Cole, a now rare if not unique apparatus whose subsequently scattered parts have recently been identified, restored and reassembled. Manuscript instructions describe how to measure the parabolic curve of a projectile ejected by the compressed air in the cylinder. The experiment is described in Francis Hauksbee's, *Experiments* (Pneumaticks, plate III, fig 1, p.17) to which Cole's accompanying letter refers. The apparatus is virtually identical to that shown in the above plate, though the supporting members are of brass and not iron as suggested by Hauksbee.

Constable's purchase of instruments to the value of £191, in the year 1757-8 from Benjamin Cole alone remains the largest and best documented collection of this firm's instruments, and provides a unique opportunity for studying their designs. The latter would be adjusted should the patron so desire.

Demonstration and so called Drawing Room pieces

Experiments using the inclined plane are also engraved in Hauksbee (plate I). The different geometric bodies there illustrated were sent to Constable by Ann Moor for the amusing rolling experiments Hauksbee had described. John Marshall charged for a model brass four wheeled carriage which could be used in conjunction with an inclined plane to demonstrate 'the absurdity of the common method of loading' - to quote Arden's Syllabus. Only the fragment of a wooden one now remains.

Models showing the latest engineering inventions were deemed essential for the philosophical cabinet. Thus the well used 'squirting' and 'continuous stream' glass models of fire engine pumps bought from Cole for £2.8.0 were also part of the equipment of the itinerant lecturer, James Ferguson.[59] Standard equipment too was the model of the pile driver designed by Valoué for driving the piled foundations for Westminster Bridge (1735). Constable's considerable interest in improving his farming methods is represented by mahogany models which include two of the then new horsedrawn implements, one of them a triple outlet seed drill as Arden mentions in his Syllabus. Suited more to the drawing room than the philosophical cabinet were the musical glasses which Constable was most eager to order from his London agent John Dunn. The latter reported their production by a Mr. Smeaton (John Smeaton F.R.S., 1724-92).[60] One glass may be a survivor but there also remain more than two octaves of the set of glass bars of a *stickador*, each bar engraved with the appropriate musical note. Mozart composed two pieces for these once fashionable sets of musical glasses.[61]

Chemistry

Constable's endeavours in Chemistry reflect a changing climate away from the above 'drawing room science' toward a more rigorous professional attitude, a change that was to have long lasting and still current consequences. In Constable's day both he and his fellow landowners in the vicinity were happy to regard science as an essential part of the education of a gentleman. One cannot discern a comparable attitude in their 19th century successors. For example, in 1763 Arden had provided Constable with a booklet of experiments entitled *On the transmutation of and production of Colour* together with the necessary pigments, for example 'dutch pink' (in fact a yellow) and 'prussian blue', which are still identifiable in their little labelled circular wooden boxes and chemicals including litmus, and tinctures of roses and violets.

In contrast, sixteen years later Constable was taking part in a subscription to aid Priestley's experiments whilst working on some of them himself. John Fothergill (1706-80) physician, naturalist, horticulturalist and founder of the Quaker school at Ackworth, suggested that four men, Theodore Jansen, Sir George Savile, William Constable and himself[62] each paid ten pounds per annum 'to aid Joseph Priestley in his experiments'; interestingly at least the latter three were all Yorkshire-men, Royal Society members, of wide ranging interests and Whigs in political inclination. Only Constable's subscription was to continue for the full ten years and was receipted annually by Priestley - 'to my experiments'. Apparatus such as a pneumatic trough, gas jars and chemicals survives to indicate that Constable experimented with gases himself.

In fact Priestley sent Constable instructions for two chemical experiments, the first, dealing with the effects of heating oxides clearly annunciates Priestley's Phlogiston theory! (phlogiston was thought to be the burning element *inside* substances capable of being burnt). The second describes the effect of heating water mixed with quick lime and compares the results with that of a volcano amidst rocks of 'calcareous substances'. Details of the apparatus required for these experiments are not given.[63] There also remains at Burton Constable the rare survival in an English cabinet, of a two foot concave mirror mounted in a 'brass Semicircle to fitt in a Pillar & Claw' for which Cole was paid £15.0.0. This could well have been used for obtaining the heat source in such chemical experiments, as well as for experimental work upon optics.[64]

Equally associated with Priestley - and put together from disparate parts on Landing 14, is number 2073 of 'Dr. Nooth's apparatus' for impregnating water with 'fixed air' (carbon dioxide), for subsequent medicinal use. The glassware was almost certainly made by William Parker, 69 Fleet Street, London, who, besides making scientific glassware such as the 'Nooth' apparatus required by Priestley,[65] also made the brilliantly light refracting chandeliers and girandoles famous in their day.

The combination of arts and science in one manufactory is similarly seen at Josiah Wedgwoods, a firm that provided high temperature thermometers for Priestley. It would not of course have seemed strange to Constable who was also a patron of Wedgwood.

Purchasing policy

No printed catalogue of John Arden or the other local instrument makers has been traced, indeed they were not often available in the mid 18th century even in London. The Marshalls must surely have worked to expert instructions either from Constable himself or his advisers such as Arden. Even the royal instrument makers, Benjamin Cole were prepared to make machines especially to Constable's specifications. The latter may have been helped in purchases from Cole by a list included in some editions of Joseph Harris *Description and Use of the Globes and the orrery*. The 1738 edition occurs in the Burton Constable library catalogue. In the case of George Adams a printed catalogue was available entitled *Micrographia Illustrata* (1749). But this also contained instructions on the use of Adam's microscopes. However for the use of a pedometer and the variation compass that Constable also bought from Adams for nine guineas, the maker included a letter of instructions with his account. In his comments on the latter instrument Adams describes how the compass is adapted for measuring the daily variations in the earth's magnetism, including adaptations of the influence of the aurora borealis and concludes 'thus far Dr. Knight', an acknowledgement to the then authority on magnetism. In fact Adams was probably selling a compass designed by Knight.[66]

Constable was also helped on a day to day basis by John Dunn, whose indefatigable searches for the curious are revealed in his correspondence. He included references to items such as the 'Adams Electric Machine' and 'Adam's Magnetic Magic' in letters of 1767, as well as more cryptic references to 'china roses' which were fireworks. The surviving letters are all from the 1760's when Constable was at his most active as a scientist.[67] Dunn himself travelled abroad and in his account of the philosophical cabinet of Prince Charles, which he had seen at Brussels, comments on the superiority of parts of the Constable cabinet. How far Constable made personal contacts with the Prince or other men of science during his Grand Tours is not wholly clear, but certainly he intended to do so. He kept up close associations with his eminent naturalist brother and the family archives indicate a connection with at least thirty other members of the Royal Society. Among these were some of the instrument makers he patronised - Edward Nairne, Peter Dollond Jnr., Jesse Ramsden and John Smeaton, while the eminent Sir Joseph Banks and Daniel Solander were seconder and proposer respectively, for Constable's election to the Royal Society in 1775. The traveller Thomas Pennant became one of Constable's suppliers and some correspondence with him is preserved in the collection of letters now at the Bodleian Library. Constable also subscribed to one of Pennant's books - among other authors. Such productive intellectual intercourse between amateurs and professionals at the Royal Society reflect a period when the same breadth of interests was shared by both to mutual benefit. However though the instruments may have been brought out of the display cabinet for experimental use, the concept of seeing them as objects of curiosity in themselves was clearly present. The instrument maker George Adams comments on the practical use of the philosophical cabinet in his introduction to *Micrographia Illustrata*, 1749, where he writes 'The study of Mathematicks is now so generally esteemed as to become a necessary part of almost every Gentleman's education'. The 'Mathematical instruments' . . . .' enable us to connect Theory with Practice and to turn what was only bare contemplation into the most substantial Uses'. He went on to apologise that the instruments lack 'superfluous Ornament' because they are for 'practical use' but that their 'Neatness may render them not unworthy of a place in the Cabinet of the Curious'. The fact that some of Constable's instruments had such ornament is surely an indication of an older fashioned view by their maker as well as of Constable's personal attitude regarding the fusion of science and art.

Such concepts of science as seen in the advertise-ments and writings of the Adams, or John and James Arden represent a transitional period in its practice and progress which is paralleled by Constable's own studies. By the end of the 18th century, as science was seen to progress so far beyond amateur interest its scope and complexity found less of a place for the gentlemen scientist, invaluable though his help had been in an earlier generation. Even though in 1775 Priestley, on the end paper of Vol.1 *On Air*, published an engraving that shows his experiments being carried out in a contemporarily furnished room, the dangerous and potentially damaging nature of his and other's experiments was of necessity to lead to the building of specialised work rooms or laboratories. Moreover, improving technology meant that such a room could be equipped with permanent services to provide heat and water, as demonstrated in the fitting out of the Royal Institution for the regular public demonstration of scientific experiments in London after 1800. An important aspect of Constable's scientific work is that it throws light on the nature of this transitional period between two eras in the history of scientific experimentation. Constable's own work benefited from the earlier approach, enabling him also to achieve sufficient perception for him to promote research that was to change the old order. Turner writes that the seeds of modern science are to be found in the cabinets of curiosity.[68] A study of the impact of cabinets such as Constables should help in the understanding of their germination.

10. *Model of a horsedrawn three furrow plough and seed drill combined.*

11. *Pneumatic trough; the kind of apparatus Joseph Priestley would have used for collecting oxygen by the displacement method which he invented. Gases passing into an inverted cylinder filled with mercury replace the latter and collect at the top of the jar. (19 inches long, made of mahogany).*

CHAPTER FIVE

NATURAL HISTORY - THE HERBARIUM

When Constable was proposed for membership of the Royal Society in 1775 he was described as 'a Gentleman deeply versed in natural history . . . .' How this epithet was achieved is to a large extent revealed in the records of his various collections which include his herbarium and his library. These endeavours can be seen as a reflection of the renaissance concept which embraces the garden as a part of a cabinet of curiosities. In this he was following the tradition promoted by the Tradescants, father and son a century earlier. Though the latter were primarily gardeners and botanists their 'Ark' at Lambeth was also crammed with non-botanical curiosities - a pattern repeated at Burton Constable.(pl.2) Through the following two centuries the balance of collections tends toward the latter but not so in Constable's case. Indeed in Constable's practical approach to botany can be seen an unusual phenomenon among the connoisseurs at any rate, in the first half of the 18th century. If they did indulge in collecting and preserving plants they rarely left a comparable record, to that surviving at Burton Constable. The exceptions include the two famous lady gardeners, the Duchess of Beaufort (1630-1714), the Duchess of Portland (d.1784), Constable's kinsman, Lord Petre (1713-1742) and the 3rd Earl of Bute (1713-92) also compiled botanical records. Another group keenly interested in these matters were not unexpectedly, doctors of medicine and many of their herbaria can be found among those collected by Sir Hans Sloane, now to be seen at the British Museum (Natural History).[69] Indeed Constable's father Cuthbert Tunstall (d.1747) was a keen naturalist and medical man; William Constable and his half brother, Marmaduke Tunstall followed in his footsteps.

Constable's plant collections

The main records of Constable's botanical work can be studied in ten volumes of the herbarium,[70] togeher with his notebook, that lists the 500 odd plants that he grew in his 'Wild flower garden', and his nurserymen's accounts. Sadly the eleven 'drawings' that hung in the north wing, made for Constable by the famous botanical artist and Linnaean, G.D. Ehret (1708-1770) who visited Burton Constable in the 1760's, were sold long ago.[71]

One may distinguish three phases in the herbarium: the first gathering phase when Constable begins to use the Linnaean system, then, though the collection was largely complete by the time of his second Grand Tour, his complete revision of that collection using the Linnaean system of binomial nomenclature, and the final phase, when collecting had diminished but accurate knowledge of nomenclature had improved.

The herbarium volumes are numbered IV, V, VI and 1-6 respectively, together with an unbound and untitled volume, the latter and "6" belonging to the third series. The specimens are generally mounted singly on the page, a practice by no means general at the time, and the pages are usually inserted loosely on to sheets of special herbarium paper so that reordering according to changing principles of classification could be effected easily. This latter practice was recommended by Linnaeus himself.[72]

The sheets of herbarium paper were stitched together into folio sized books, leather spined between boards, the appropriate volume number being tooled onto the spine. The inside cover of several volumes contains Constable's bookplate. Each volume holds between 100 and 200 species. Found separately were a number of mounted specimens placed between the pages of an unbound printed book.

Classification of plants

The three different series of herbaria were all ordered according to the Linnaean sexual system, where plants are grouped according to the number of stamens in the flowers and subclassified according to the number of styles. This classification was published in the first edition of *Systema natura* (1735) and popularised with colour illustrations by G.D. Ehret in the following year.[73] The reception of Linnaeus's principles in this country has been fully analysed by W.T. Stearn.[74] As far as can be discerned Constable's is among the first of the English collections to take up Linnaeus's classifications. This ability to perceive the significance of such advances in science and then to adapt his work to them is a characteristic of Constable.

Only volumes IV-VI survive of the earliest series. The dates revealed in volum IV range from 1742 to 1752. Plants are labelled with long descriptive polynomials each with many synonyms and their sources, which derive from books in the Library. Volume IV starts with class 19 of the Linnaean system, - basically the Compositae. Unusually the first source quoted for nomenclature in this volume is *Hortus Cliffortianus* (1738) - within which many of the plants could be identified. Here Linnaeaus used his sexual system of classification for the first time in an arrangement of a catalogue of the garden plants of his patron, (and Constable's distant kinsman), George Clifford of Haartenkamp, Holland. Often but by no means always, the synonyms quoted are also copied from *Hortus Cliffortianus*. Indeed it has been suggested that Linnaeus may have been stimulated to devise a new system whilst preparing this volume,[75] copies of which were only obtained by gift from Clifford. Constable was thus fortunate to obtain a copy,[76] which he then put into immediate use. However he did not carry out the labelling work unaided, for the labels are in a variety of hands though all of volume IV, some of V and the whole of 6 are in the same hand. Revision slips occur on most pages, usually giving at least the generic name of the new binomials and sometimes the English name as well.

Preparation of specimens

In a letter of 1st July 1764, from one of Constable's advisers and suppliers of curiosities, Mendes da Costa, the latter writes that "I have just left Mr. Sherwood and his family who present their compliments to you. Mr. Sherwood is extremely busy pasting the plants on paper according to your desire and hopes to send them you in next Monday's carrier".[77]

Mr. James Sherwood of Devonshire Street, London, is introduced to meetings of the Royal Society on several occasions in the 1750's and is mentioned in other letters by a da Costa. However the hand of volume IV is only discernible in volume 6 of the books that are post 1763. The practice of sending plants to a specialist for labelling is described in one of Rousseau's letters to Mme Delessert.

Constable's horticultural circle; provenance of plants in Vol. IV

Though it is uncertain who the scribe is for Volume IV, it is in several ways the most complete work, for not only does it contain a wide range of garden, native and French plants but the labels mostly include the date and the provenance. The latter descriptions throw light not only on Constable's botanical travels around London and Paris, but also the circle of eminent naturalists and gardeners with whom he associated.

Of garden plants with acknowledged origin, the most, 10, came from Thorndon, Lord Petre's famous garden; though by 1745-1746 when they were sent, Lord Robert James Petre (1713-42) was no longer alive. The plants not unexpectedly also include recent introductions from Eastern North America, for example No.18 is *Rudbeckia foliis compositis integris*. (polynomial) *Royen* (authority).[80] Page number 181.

Here Royen had to be used as the authority because the introduction in 1737 was too late for inclusion in *Hortus Cliffortianus*. From Lord Petre's famous hothouses came the specimen, *Passiflora caerulea* and there is also a sample of Petre's famous variegated hornbeam. Two West Indian plants - *Sisyrinchium bermudianum* and the newly introduced *Polypodium aureum* (1742) were sent from 'Mr. Gordon's garden at Mile End'. James

Gordon (1708?-80) had been Petre's gardener before setting up his nursery at Mile End in 1738, and he became known for his exceptional skills in the propagation and culture of new introductions such as the camellia. Constable bought from him the rare and newly reintroduced 'Andrachne', *(Arbutus andrachne)* which cost 2 guineas in 1762. Much more commonplace at that time was the cornflower or 'blew bottles' supplied by the vice president of the Royal Society the well known microscopist, Henry Baker.

There are 18 plants gathered around Paris, mostly dated 1742, when Constable visited France with his tutor, Dr. Molyneux. The finds included three orchids and the royal fern *Osmunda regalis* found 'in a Bogg hill going from Montmorency to St. Prit 6 leagues from Paris'. 'English black maidenhair' had been retrieved 'from the walls of our (?) old bason in the Park of Meudon nigh Paris June 1742'. Thirty wild plants have stations around London, many from Hampstead Heath. The six specimens sent by the botanist John Hill, (1716?-75) in 1746, may well have been commercially supplied plants for at this time he was supplementing his income as a pharmacist by supplying collectors with dried specimens. Four of his plants are mosses, and it may well be that nos. 129-136 are mosses also sent by Hill since they came at the same time and with provenance around London, again mainly Hampstead Heath. Interest in mosses was at that time in its infancy, Dillenius having just published the first full work on the subject *Historia Muscorum* in 1741. Another eminent botanist, Dr. Butner, provided two rare specimens which were the result of an expedition to Wales in 1751. They were *Sedum fosteriana* from the much botanised St. Vincent's rock and *Narthecium ossifragum*.

Thomas Knowlton, 1691-1781

Constable's interest in mountain plants seems to have been furthered by Thomas Knowlton, head gardener to Lord Burlington and subsequently to the Duke of Devonshire. Knowlton was in a good position to bring his unusual plants to Burton Constable as he had been engaged to build the new greenhouse complex on the West Lawn there in 1757, and the menagerie in 1760. In the case of two plants, rice and 'Rapunculus Rampion - I am not sure if it is right' *(Trachelium caeruleum)* the labels state they are from Thomas Knowlton - who also kept his own collection of dried plants. The recent publication by the late Miss Blanche Henrey, *No Ordinary gardener Thomas Knowlton 1691-1781*, 1986 reveals Knowlton's keen interest in the unusual. In a letter to Samuel Brewer he writes 'I shall soon (write) to Mr. Collinson & Catesby wch will then transm(it) to me all ye news of ye curiuose things wch Like yrself I am always well pleased to Read & heare of'[81] Miss Henrey also comments on Knowlton's generosity with seeds and plants.

Some of the introductions of Mark Catesby (1682-1749) in Volume VI and in the second series may thus come through the Knowlton connection. Some of the latter's special favourites turn up in Constable's Herbarium. (Second series) For example there is his own introduction the 'Deare Double nasturtium' frequently mentioned because of the difficulty of growing it. Another Knowlton plant is the blue pimpernel, *Anagallis monelli*.

'Curiosities' and 'oddments' in Vol. V and VI

Volume V is a heterogenous collection of plants in no special order and variously labelled, frequently with revisions using Hudson's *Flora Anglica* (1762) as a reference work. Plants of special interest include *Tradescantia virginiana* from 'my own garden 1745', the fairly new moss Provence rose and the rare *Pedicularis palustris* with the very detailed provenance 'from Hampstead Heath the Back of the long rooms'.

Volume VI differs from all the others in being devoted to ornamental trees, fruit trees, shrubs, many obtained from the eastern states of North America and connected with the plant hunter Mark Catesby (1682-1749). They are well preserved, often varnished, in no classifed order, and with no dates.

The labels on these plants are in various hands not

seen in any other volume, often giving only English names but with the characteristic later revisions.

In 1759 Constable bought a large number of American plants then so much in vogue from the nursery of Christopher Gray, eleven of this list being preserved in volume VI.[82] In 1763 he obtained seeds of American plants 'just arrived' from Lee and Kennedy.[83] One also wonders whether some of Constable's rarer specimens are the nurseryman's samples. In the case of several trees, 'red twigged lime' and 'ash leav'd maple' and 'evergreen oak' ancient plants are still to be found growing at Burton Constable. The infrequently planted ash-leaved maple still forms part of a hedge tree in the 'stove' garden created c.1772. Surprisingly perhaps, there is no record of Constable supporting plant hunting expeditions as many contemporary amateur botanists did. For example both Lord Petre and John Fothergill are known to have supported John Bartram in Eastern North America[84] and specimens Bartram sent to the former are preserved in his Hortus Siccus[85] while some of Catesby collections are preserved in the Sloane collection and in Sherard's herbarium at Oxford.

Thomas Kyle - the fruit gardener

The twenty specimens of fruit trees are also mainly curiosities, for example the unusual "twice flowering pear" and "Macalet cherry" (the mahaleb cherry, *Prunus mahaleb*) which was grown for its perfumed wood. Both appear in the undated James Gordon catalogue at the Lindley library as does the 'apple bearing rose' here also represented. There are too the double flowered forms of pear, wild cherry and plum, supplied by the nurserymen Perfects of Pontefract. Between 1758 and 1768 the orchards and glasshouses were cared for by the distinguished Scottish gardener, Thomas Kyle who was later to publish *A treatise on the management of peaches and nectarines* (1783) (bought by Constable in 1788). In 1763 he had been commissioned by Constable to write a report on the latest agricultural improvements in East Anglia and on aspects of horticulture and landscape design at various estates in the Home Counties.[86] It can

be shown that he assisted Constable in preparation of the second series of the herbarium.

The use of the Linnaean classification 1763

Volumes 1-5 are systematically put together to display the new system the legend on the title page reading:-
Hortus Siccus
ubi
Plantae Distributae Sunt
Secundum
Linnai Systema Sexuale
apud Burton Constable
In Cava Deira
Anno
Ab Incarnatione
Christi
1763

The start of each of the new 24 classes and orders is marked with an identifying label, though not all orders are represented. Each page is numbered in the top right hand corner with the class and order numbers for the relevant specimen in accordance with Constable's newly purchased second edition of Linnaeus *Species plantarum*, 1763, and using its new binomial nomenclature now generally recognised as the starting point of modern botanical nomenclature.[87]

Most frequently in the first five volumes the labelling hand can be identified as the Head Gardener's, Thomas Kyle, who also wrote the classification slips and then revision slips in these and other volumes. There are occasional commentaries in English by Constable. The latter's hand with its characteristic backward 'e' and written in copperplate, can also be identified. With the starter's enthusiasm he labelled all the specimens in volume 1, and a good proportion of those in volume 2. Throughout there are frequent page references to the first Linnaean British flora, Hudson's *Flora Anglica* (1762) newly purchased by Constable. Occasionally references, occur to older 17th century authors - such as Johnson (Johnson's edition of Gerard's *Herbal* 1632) and to Park

(John Parkinson *Theatrum botanicum*, 1640). In two instances Vaillant *Botanicum Parisiense* (1727) was used with reference to illustrations of *Seseli carvifolia* and *Sagina erecta*. Vaillant was exceptional for the period in providing illustrated reference material, an additional aid to identification for these two rarer plants. The latter three volumes were almost certainly a part of Cuthbert Constable's library.

There are signs that Kyle is learning as he goes along, for sometimes his labels give pre-Linnaean generic names as in the pre-1768 editions of Phillip Miller's *Dictionary* and to these he adds the English descriptive name. The generic name, sometimes attributed to *Linn* is clearly an afterthought. In volume 6 and the unbound volume, which cover only the first 12 Linnaean classes, binomial nomenclature is much more complete but the scribe could be the same as in the older volume IV. The latest date is 1777 - (deduced by a reference to William Curtis *Flora Londinensis,* part 8). Presumably these two volumes represent a third improved attempt at a thorough representation of the Linnaean classes.

Mounting

It would be of interest to know how the high standard of preservation was achieved. In two specimens the normally rather fugitive blue is particularly well preserved, *Veronica bellidoides* and *Delphinium* commonly called Bee Larkspur and these and most other specimens were clearly mounted with an eye to elegance of effect.

This aesthetic approach however is quite different from that of the Hortus Siccus of George Clifford[88] where plant stems are artistically arranged and placed in cut-out prints of classical urns and the labels written within an especially printed baroque cartouche. This contrast can be paralleled by the stiff formality of the baroque garden and the more natural forms adopted by the landscape gardeners of Constable's day indeed Kyle reused paper, making loose labels as noted above. The few dates included in volumes 1-5 show that the material was in the main collected between 1763-1769. Kyle left in the latter year.

Plant sources

Provenance for the plants can be deduced for many of Constable's own garden specimens, including those few labelled 'from the greenhouse', on a label slit to fit round the plant that had been cut by the head gardener.

The numbers given to the plants in the herbarium can in over 100 cases be matched to the numbered list in Constable's notebook entitled: A Catalogue of Plants upon the North Border in the Stove Garden those Mark'd G are plants found near the Garden house. H for plants found in Holderness. Of the 500 or so plants there listed, 240 were marked as from Holderness, many in the herbarium. Some of the others, partly foreign can be found among the accounts of the Perfects of Pontefract and Telfords of York. An account dated 1772 from James Byres, Constable's cicerone and agent in Rome, indicates a continuing development of Constable's botanic garden though this list is not now traceable through the herbarium. Byres notes '57 different parcels of Seeds from the Botanic Gardens' and '21 different parcels do. from the Borghese Gardens'.[89] Up to this period the stove and botanic garden newly built in 1757, had been conveniently situated on the north side of West Lawn, that is immediately adjacent to the house. It was not a part of the present kitchen garden complex, started only c.1772.[90] The 1757 plan retained at Burton Constable revealingly shows a Master's room in the greenhouse of that date.

Holderness plants

Exceptionally the specimen of *Viburnum opulus* is annotated 'from George Caley's moor'. The Caleys have long been tenant farmers on the estate. However the list for Holderness derived from Constable's notebook of the wild flower garden, which can be dated to the 1760's contains many 'first' records for the area. Indeed there are few earlier records. John Ray's *Synopsis*, 3rd ed. 1724, has *Lysimachia thyrsiflora* which has not been found since, and *Carum carvi* that Constable did get. In 1729, Thomas Knowlton noted three Hornsea plants to Samuel

Brewer, another keen grower of British plants, *Cakile maritima, Honkenya peploides* and *Salsola kali*, none of them in the herbarium. At Atwick near Hornsea lived the Rev. William Whytehead who prepared a herbarium containing many local plants between the years 1757 and 1817 latterly preserved at Hull University. He in turn preserved 34 plants located from William Constable's garden - which he termed in one case 'botanic'. In the 1790's Robert Teesdale junior, head gardener at Castle Howard worked on the first long list for the area.[91]

It covered the Wolds and Holderness, particularly Hornsea and the Humber Bank, including species found in Constable's herbarium.

The above records deserve more study but it is clear that some of the fine Holderness specimens in Constable's herbarium are now rare or extinct. For example Herb Paris, *Paris quadrifolia*, has not been located in Holderness since 1956, and Saintfoin, *Onobrychis viciifolia*, an escape from cultivation first recorded in the Wolds c.1740[92] and recommended as a crop by Kyle has now also gone, as has woad, *Isatis tinctoria*. Other plants preserved but now uncommon are darnel grass, *Lolium temulentum*, 'white horehound', *Marrubium vulgare*, 'Pseudomelianthemum', *Agrostemma githago*, 'Corn Marigold', *Chrysanthemum segetum*, and *Thalictrum majus*. Maritime plants in the Burton Constable herbarium include sea lavender, wild carrot, thrift, *Artemisia maritima, Scirpus maritimus* and *Glaux maritima*. The latter four are in Teesdale's list which further includes *Eriophoron polystachion* and *Bromus secalinus* and likewise available in the Constable herbarium.

Northern mountain plants

Specimens of *Galium boreale, Littorella uniflora, Parnassia palustris, Eryngium alpinum, Myosotis alpestris, Arenaria laricifolia* and *Ligusticum scotisum* are evidence that an interest in mountain plants was maintained. *Ligusticum scoticum* grows mainly on the coast of Scotland,[93] *Cornus suecica* was also a very restricted, a plant much prized by Knowlton - who had great difficulty in obtaining it.[94] It grew in the wild flower garden. The latter is down as *Chaemaepericlymenum* dwarf herbaceous honeysuckle G.93 in Constable's notebook. Knowlton searched successfully in the wild for Herb Christopher (*Actaea spicata*), Astragalus perennial milk vetch (*Astragalus danicus*) and Andromeda (*Andromeda polifolia*) all also in the herbarium and grown in the wild flower garden. Knowlton was very anxious to raise the botanical and horticultural standards of his northern patrons for, as he commented in a letter to Richard Richardson jun. of Bierley in 1750/51 'the onely gardens in ye northern parts is Orford & Bierly they Indeed abound with many of ye wonders of ye creation'. By distributing his unusual finds to the cognescenti he was clearly furthering this not unfamiliar aim.

Growing specialist plants together, was a relatively innovative venture and the provision of rocks and other special requirements for mountain plants had barely been considered. Knowlton comments on Richard Richardson jun. practice in this respect in 1763. There were: 'plants that were scattered in yr. rocks as they were likely places to grow upon and be so uncommon a natural ornament to ye same'.[95] Constable's associate, Dr. John Fothergill (1712-80), an early specialist in alpines who then lived at Upton, Essex, seems to have grown his plants in pots.[96] A hundred years later James Niven's large and healthy alpine collection (lately at Hull Botanic Garden) was still considered something of a novelty.[97]

Exotics

The collection of tender plants represented can also often be traced to Constable's collaboration with Thomas Knowlton, including economic plants such as 'gramen pinnatum from Mr. Knowlton' which has been identified as rice (*Orrhiza sativa*) as well as a specimen of the sugar plant (*Saccharum officinale*). There are two recently introduced timber trees - 'Haematoxylon' (*Haematoxylum campechianum*) and 'Citharexylum', the former used as a black dye for textiles in Jamaica, the latter in making musical instruments. Striking among the ornamentals is 'Catesby's Hellebore' 'Linadorum Linn'

(*Calopogon pulchellum R.Br*). Of this plant Miller comments in 1752, 'Purple bastard Hellebore with a tuberose root - sent from Bahama Islands by Peter Collinson since been distributed to many curious persons in England. This is a very fine Plant, and deserves a Place in the Stove, because it produces a most beautiful Spike of purple Flowers every Year.[98] Thus Constable seems to have had the opportunity to grow in his stove, one of the earliest exotic orchids to be introduced into this country. Another stove plant 'Erythrina thick-rooted from Carolina' (*Erythrina herbacea*) is a plant also introduced by Catesby and here shown with a flower. There is a flowering specimen of 'Turnera ulmifolia', (1733) and 'Hura the sandbox tree' both part of a large collections sent to Chelsea Physic Garden by William Houston from the West Indies c.1731 as is the then rare 'Rivinia humilis', the Bloodberry from the West Indies. African plants include 'Mallow in the gr.house malva shrubby afr'' (*Malva capensis?*)(intro. 1727), 'Triangular-leaved aloe (*Aloe triangularis*) (1732) and 'Halleria African fly honeysuckle' (*H. lucida L.*)(1752). An intriguing and then recent introduction from Madagascar was the handsomely pressed pink flowered *Catharanthus roseus* (1758), first cultivated in this country by Knowlton before 1756 and now grown in the tropics for its alkaloids. Others from Africa such as Mesembryanthemums, 'Hermannia with a lavender leaf' Lesser Torch thistle (*Aporocactus flagelliformis*), 'Amber tree' (*Anthospermum aethiopicum*) (1696) 'Geranium afr. shrubby smelling like baum' seem to have been introduced into Europe over a longer period.

Hot house plants from Asia include *Basella rubra*, Climbing Malabar Nightshade (1757) and *Sophora tomentosa*, first grown by Phillip Miller at Chelsea Physic Garden in 1739.

Hardy foreign plants

The specimens again reveal the popularity of the new and novel introduced American plants. For example 'Azalea viscosa' (1734) 'Dodecatheon' (reintroduced 1745), Clethra Longifolia, 'Polemonium with a creeping root' (*Polemonium reptans*) and 'Dahoon Holly' (*Ilex cassine*) and 'Clethra - short spiked' (*Clethra paniculata*), all species introduced by Peter Collinson who had obtained them from Mark Catesby in the 1720's for cultivation at Mill Hill.[99]

Nurserymen's bills

Some certainty exists about the secondary origin of some of the annual cultivated plants because of surviving seed bills in the Constable papers. Thus the fairly recently introduced plant chinese aster (*Callistephus chinensis*) which Knowlton called a 'gloryous plant', can be found on several bills from the Pontefract nurseryman Perfects, together with 'the China Pink' (*Dianthus chinensis*), 'Egyptian Mignonette' (*Reseda odorata*) (1752) various stocks and the tender 'sensitive plant' (*Mimosa pudica*) all also in the herbarium. Perfects, on one occasion sent a free parcel of paeonies and volume three has a fine specimen of 'Paeonia flore rubra pleno', much like a modern cultivar.

Horticultural specialities

Double flowering plants were at once curiosities and high fashion during the middle of the 18th century. Most of the forms in the herbarium, are still common today such as double marsh marigold, double columbine, double almond and wild cherry. Less common in current cultivation are the double pilewort and ladies smock. The other notable variant found in contemporary decoration is the variegated leaf. Samples of the latter are: 'Angelica', 'Spiraea meadow sweet', 'vinca with white flowers and striped leaves' and 'Phalaris arundinacea'. The range of variegated plants in the Duchess of Beaufort's collection is commented on by Britten and Dandy.[100] It is notable that this older fashion is seen to continue in Constable's choice of plants and these fashions have been revived in our own day.

Conclusion

The overall approach to taxonomy as revealed in the three series of herbaria indicates Constable's rapid perception of Linnaeus' new principles of classification and nomenclature, as they developed in successive publications.

Here Constable was an innovator for it can be shown that in general, English botanists did not use Linnaean principles till well after the establishment of the binomial nomenclature with the publication of *Species plantarum* in 1753 and *Genera plantarum* a year later.[101] In this he cannot have been helped by his friend and consultant Thomas Knowlton for the latter was not a Linnaean, nor by Kyle who was clearly learning as he went along aided by Constable. Knowlton among others, did however play an important part in realising Constable's clear aim to make and preserve a botanic garden - a feature that was to reach its peak of popularity in the earlier 19th century.[102]

His careful preparation of the botanic garden catalogue as well as in 1789 an index for *Flora Londinensis* reveals something of Constables depth of botanical interest.

This one can see in Constable's endeavours both the attitude of the pure 'Cabinet collector' and the scientist who seeks an understanding of the ordered pattern to be discovered among the infinite variety of natural species. The impact of such Englishmen;s botanic gardens on the progress of botany is a subject meriting further study. Certainly Constable's successor Edward Sheldon made a contribution when he subscribed £20 to the new botanic garden at Linnaeus Street, Hull in April 1813!

Note. The botanical nomenclature here used follows that of the *Royal Horticultural Society Dictionary*. Where plant names occur within inverted commas they are copied directly from the herbaria and not necessarily checked as accurate.

Much help has been given in identification of species, and for this I am particularly indebted to Arthur Chater, Roy Vickery and the ever helpful staff at the British Museum (Natural History) General Herbarium, Alan Mitchell, Christine Thompson, John Harvey and Derrick Boatman.

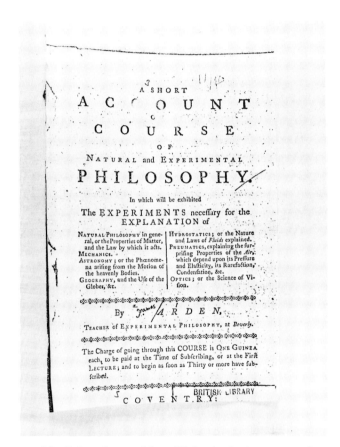

12. Printed pamphlet of John Arden's course of experiments, elaborated and published by his son James.

13. (above) Orangery with coade stone ornaments;
a greenhouse for exotic and tender plants.

14. (right) Fossil cabinet probably made by the
estate carpenter.

CHAPTER SIX

WILLIAM CONSTABLE'S 'FOSSIL CABINET'

In addition to his collection of scientific instruments, William Constable assembled several considerable 'cabinets' of 'natural curiosities' or - in modern terminology - substantial collections of geological, botanical and zoological specimens. His geological collection or 'fossil cabinet' possesses two features which render it of particular interest to the historian of the natural sciences in Great Britain. First, the collection is substantially intact and, with the exception of 201 specimens generously presented to Hull City Museums by Mr. J.R. Chichester-Constable in 1966, still stored in its, apparently purpose-built, cabinet at Burton Constable Hall. It is thus an unusually well-preserved example of an eighteenth century geology 'cabinet' - in the fullest sense of the term. Second, with the notable exception of a small number of specimens collected locally by William Constable himself, a great proportion of the collection was acquired from the well-known naturalist, antiquary and dealer in 'natural curiosities' Emanuel Mendes da Costa (1717-1791).

There are however important contributions from Henry Baker FRS[103] and Thomas Pennant,[104] traveller and naturalist.

The, several hundred, specimens of rocks, minerals and fossils which make up William Constable's geological collection are, as noted above, mostly still housed in what appears to be their original wooden cabinet. The cabinet measures 43 inches by 43 inches and has a maximum height of 56 inches. Each of two opposing sides of the cabinet accommodates thirty-two storage drawers, each bank of drawers comprising eight of small size, fourteen of medium and ten of large size. The cabinet, although generally well-made, is noticeably lacking in the fine exterior finish and fittings generally found in eighteenth century domestic furniture of high quality. Instead, it conveys an impression of functional solidity and could well have been manufactured locally

by a skilled joiner, rather than by a cabinet maker *sensu stricto*. The drawers lack any system of internal division and the geological specimens for the most part lie loose within them. Although this situation is initially suggestive of disorder resulting from two centuries of comparative neglect, the fact that many specimens are still wrapped in their original paper labels, precisely as they were first received from Mendes da Costa, might be taken to indicate that the present, somewhat casual, mode of storage of the collection is not so markedly different to that which obtained during William Constable's lifetime.

The great majority of the geological specimens comprising the surviving 'fossil cabinet' of William Constable were, as has been noted above, supplied by the famous (and infamous!) Emanuel Mendes da Costa, 'that wayward Hebrew genius . . . . whose scientific enthusiasm atoned for less honourable traits of character'.[105] Born in 1717, da Costa was a Jewish merchant of French and Portuguese extraction, whose forbears had settled in England during the seventeenth century. An enthusiastic naturalist, geologist and antiquary, whose principal scientific interests lay in conchology and palaeontology, da Costa appears to have been a man of considerable intellectual ability and personal charm. By the time of his election to Fellowship of the Royal Society, in 1747, he seems to have won the respect (and, in some cases, friendship) of many of the most distinguished scientists and antiquaries of the eighteenth century, including Sir Hans Sloane, Martin Folkes and William Stukely. Da Costa's sponsors for his election to the Royal Society (who included Martin Folkes, then President of the Society) described him as "a Gentleman well skilled in Philosophical Learning and Natural Knowledge, particularly in what relates to the Mineral and Fossil parts of the Creation." Five years later, in 1752, da Costa was also elected a Fellow of the Society of Antiquaries. He amassed large and valuable collections, particularly of shells and geological specimens, and was, by 1761, able to declare that his collection of 'fossils' was "reckoned equal, if not superior, to any private one in England" (Allen, 1976, p33). Da Costa, however, was not merely a scientific dilettante and collector: he published his first book, *A Natural History of Fossils*, in 1757 and, two decades later, produced the two works for which he is better known, *Elements of Conchology* (1776) and *British Conchology* (1778). It was during the two decades that elapsed between the publication of his geological treatise and the publication of his conchological books that the events which led to da Costa's social and - albeit to a lesser extent - scientific downfall occurred. In 1763, da Costa was appointed to the salaried post of Clerk to the Royal Society. During the four years he spent in this position, he managed to embezzle the sum - enormous by eighteenth century standards - of almost fifteen hundred pounds from the funds of the Society. Once the theft was discovered, retribution was swift and thorough. In December, 1767, da Costa was formally dismissed from his post. In May, 1768, the Society of Antiquaries expelled him from its ranks by reason of his 'infamous conduct' and, on 9th November 1768, he was finally committed to the King's Bench Prison at St. George's Fields. Here, da Costa was to spend the next four years.[106] He was released from prison on 8th October 1772, but the remaining nineteen years of his life were apparently spent struggling to make a living, largely without the patronage and support which he might once have expected, by writing, lecturing and dealing in shells and geological specimens. He died in 1791, the same year as his erstwhile customer William Constable, at the age of seventy-four. It is sad but given human nature perhaps inevitable that Emanuel Mendes da Costa's scientific abilities and achievements should have been overshadowed, in popular memory at least, by the more lurid aspects of his life and career. Still, as Whitehead (1977) has noted, 'to earn a respected place in both the Society of Antiquaries and the Royal Society was not, in the eighteenth century, an uncommon achievement; but to be then expelled from the one and sent to prison by the other

is altogether rare!'

The principal documentary evidence linking Emanuel Mendes da Costa and William Constable (and providing details of their relationship as fellow 'fossilists') consists of a series of ten letters currently housed in the Humberside County Record Office at Beverley. These letters, written by da Costa to Constable between 1st July 1760 and 27th January, 1761, illustrate in some detail the manner in which William Constable built up his 'fossil cabinet' and also facilitate an assessment of Constable as a student of 'natural curiosities'. A brief review of the contents of the letters, all of which were written from London and addressed to William Constable at Burton Constable Hall, is therefore given below. One preliminary note is, perhaps, necessary. The term 'fossil' did not acquire its modern, restricted, meaning, 'the remains of, or traces of the activity of, a living organism, buried by natural processes and subsequently permanently preserved', until the first half of the nineteenth century. Both da Costa and Constable use the term in its earlier, more literal, sense to designate 'something which is dug up' and therefore apply it to minerals and rocks, as well as to fossils in the modern sense of the word.

The first of the ten letters from da Costa to Constable (1st July 1760) commences with the former's acknowledgement of the latter's order for 'a collection of fossils'. The order appears to have been relayed to da Costa by a Mr. Sherwood, who had evidently also been the means by which da Costa, as a potential supplier of geological material, had originally been brought to Constable's attention. Da Costa goes on to inform Constable that he has, the previous Saturday, despatched to Burton Constable 'a deal box well and carefully packed . . . containing the collection of fossils, 300 in number'. The 'fossils' appear to have been packed and labelled in an exemplary manner: 'each one is pack't up in a paper apart, Mark't with the number on the outside, and within, with the fossil, each one has its label, with notice of what it is and its number again . . . .' As has already been noted, many of da Costa's handwritten labels still survive attached to, or otherwise associated with, the specimens with which they were originally despatched to William Constable.

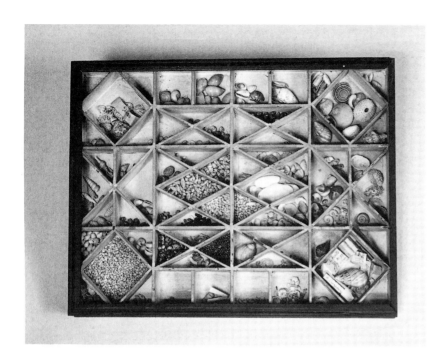

15. *Parterre of shells from Mendes da Costa.*

16. *Dried fish specimen mounted on stout paper.*

Da Costa concludes his letter of 1st July 1760 by encouraging Constable to be industrious in his 'searches after Nature' and by soliciting further orders, should Constable 'want any more fossils, any Seashells, Corals or other Natural productions.' Enclosed with the letter was a detailed list of the 'fossils' despatched by da Costa. Fortunately, this manuscript list also survives in the Humberside County Record Office. It is headed *Catalogue of fossils Sold to William Constable Esq., At Burton Constable near Hull in Yorkshire, and sent by the Lincoln Carrier 28th June 1760*. The 300 geological specimens listed, which almost all derive from the countries of the British Isles and mainland Europe, are divided by da Costa into two principal categories. The first of these, 'Native fossils or real Productions of the Earth', comprises those specimens which a modern geologist would describe as minerals and rocks. These are divided by da Costa into 'Earths', 'Stones of Strata', 'Flints, Agats, Jaspers & c', 'Talcs, Micas, Asbesti & c', 'Incrustations, Spars and Crystals', 'Sands', 'Bitumens, Sulphers, and Salts', 'Pyrites, Marcasites, Mock Ore and samples of veins', 'Semimetals', 'Gold Ores', 'Silver Ores', 'Copper Ores', 'Tin Ores', 'Lead Ores', 'Iron Ores'. The specimens falling into the second of da Costa's two main categories - 'Extraneous fossils, or Parts of Animals and Vegetables buried in the Earth: Diluvian remains' - are fossils in the modern sense of the term. Da Costa's list of 'Extraneous fossils' is divided into sections headed 'Fossil Vegetables', 'Bivalves and Multivalves of all kinds', 'Univalves of all kinds', 'Ammonitae and Nautili', 'Coralloids or Fossil Corals', 'Parts of Crustaceous Animals' and 'Parts of fish and Quadrupeds'. Item 278 on da Costa's list ('A *Hippocephaloides* or *Cuneites* from Oxfordshire') is almost certainly the interestingly-labelled specimen of the bivalve *Myophorella* whose historical significance has already been discussed by Boyd and Credland.[107]

The second of the ten letters under consideration is dated 22nd July 1760. It is clear from the contents of this letter that William Constable had, at some point during the three weeks prior to its being written, communicated to da Costa (via Mr. Sherwood - see above 'Herbarium')

both an invitation to visit Burton Constable and a series of questions regarding the geology of eastern Yorkshire. With respect to the former, da Costa thanks Constable for his 'generous invitation' but implies that he (da Costa) is unlikely to visit Yorkshire: 'I am afraid I am now become of the Oyster tribe, fixed to my dwelling in this great Metropolis'. With respect to the geology of East Yorkshire, da Costa recommends that Constable pay particular attention to the 'Bowlder stones' to be found on the coast of Holderness. The manner in which these are described leaves no doubt that da Costa is referring to glacial erratic boulders, eroded from the boulder-clay cliffs of Holderness by the sea. It is thus interesting to note that he, quite correctly, regarded them as having been transported to Holderness from elsewhere - even though he made the, perfectly understandable, mistake of regarding the sea, rather than glacial ice, as the agency of transport ('. . . . they are brought by the Sea from other parts').

Da Costa's third letter to William Constable, dated 14th August 1760, commences with a request that Constable communicate with him directly ('at the Bank Coffee House, by the Bank of England, London') rather than continuing to do so through the agency of Mr. Sherwood. After a brief exhortation to Constable to persevere in hunting for fossils - even in the 'high and earthy' sea-cliffs of Holderness where the 'earthy particles are too lax to preserve them well' - da Costa goes on to note that he has just despatched three groups of specimens to Burton Constable. These comprise a collection of corals 'purchased by Mr. Sherwood for William Constable Esq., at the price of ten guineas', a collection of 170 shells from which Constable may choose the specimens he desires and four examples of 'Stones cut and Polish'd'. Lists of the corals, shells and 'polished stones' (complete with the prices asked) are appended to the letter.

In the next letter of the series available to the present writer, which is dated 9th September 1760, da Costa notes that Constable has retained shells to the value of £22.12.0d from the collection of 170 specimens previously sent to him 'on approval' and has returned the remainder of the collection. He has also purchased all four of the 'polished stones' sent to him, at a cost of £1.13.0d, making a total (including the cost of the ten-guineas-worth of corals) of £34.15.0d. Da Costa further notes Constable's expressed desire to bring his expenditure up to the round sum of fifty guineas 'by employing the remainder £17.15.0d in polish'd stones' and informs him that he (da Costa) has, accordingly, despatched twenty-two such specimens to Burton Constable. A full list of these twenty-two specimens, with prices totalling £16.17.6d, is given in the letter. Most of the remainder of the letter is devoted to the discussion of various geological and conchological topics (Constable seems regularly to have 'bombarded' da Costa with questions relating to 'fossils' and shells) but it also includes an interesting proposal by da Costa, which is worth quoting in full:

'Now, Sir, permit me in consequence of your searches to propose to you the following, *viz*, to send me an Invoice of all the different fossils you have found, with Accurate Notices. Large or Ample specimens if you please, two or three of (each) kind, and keep by you tallying specimens. Then when I receive them, I can.. .. characterise every kind to you, note to you their particular species, and all other information, which you then can enter in your Catalogue, which will not only be instruction to us both, but great Additions to our Cabinets. But I continue with my proposal, that in return for the specimens you send me, I will send you an equal value in any Natural Curiosities you may desire, but chiefly in foreign fossils.'

As D.E. Allen has pointed out, da Costa had, by the middle of the eighteenth century, built up a nationwide network of correspondents from whom he regularly obtained both geological specimens and information. The, rather curiously-worded, passage quoted above would appear to be an invitation to William Constable to join this network.

It is clear that William Constable did, indeed, send 'fossils' collected in East Yorkshire to da Costa for identification, for twenty-two such specimens are commented upon by da Costa in the fifth letter of the series under discussion, which is dated 1st November 1760.

In this fifth letter, da Costa also impresses upon Constable the importance of recording accurately the locality from which each geological specimen has been collected; it seems that no fewer than twenty-one of the twenty-two 'fossils' despatched to da Costa by Constable were without any locality data! There is a frustrating lack of details of provenance among the botanised specimens too.

The sixth letter in the series, dated 25th November 1760, consists largely of da Costa's identifications of, and comments upon, a further series of specimens sent him by William Constable. However, not all of the specimens were from East Yorkshire and they may not, therefore, have been of Constable's own collecting.

The seventh and eighth letters from da Costa to Constable, which are dated 16th December 1760 and 18th December 1760 respectively, are here considered together, for they actually form two parts of a single communication. The essence of this communication is that da Costa has despatched to Burton Constable a large collection of (165) 'natural curiosities' in the hope that some, at least, will prove of interest. A lengthy catalogue of these 'curiosities' - which include geological, botanical and zoological specimens - is included, together with a price list. One of the items in the catalogue is worthy of special note because it was to be the cause of some little acrimony on the part of William Constable. The catalogue entry for this specimen (Item 164) reads: 'The *Lapis Crucifer* or Cross Stone, which I get at Great Expense from St. James de Compostella in Spain; where the devotees of your religion buy them to transmit to all parts of the Catholic Church. I had four pieces, the other three were bad, but this I think is as fine as ever I saw, and such are very scarce. I leave to you to value it as you like, or if you please to Accept it.' No price is marked for this specimen.

The communication formed by the seventh and eighth letters ends with da Costa's suggestions as to how Constable might best arrange the 'fossils' in his cabinet.

The ninth, and penultimate, letter in the series is dated 30th December 1760. Da Costa begins by lamenting the fact that Constable has chosen specimens to the value of only fifteen guineas from the (possibly unsolicited) collection of 'natural curiosities' sent to him earlier that month. Most of the remainder of the letter appears to be a response to an earlier letter sent by Constable on 26th December, accusing da Costa of asking extravagant prices for certain of his specimens. In his defence of his pricing policy, da Costa displays a curious blend of reason, spirit and extreme obsequiousness. The antepenultimate paragraph of da Costa's letter of 30th December is of particular interest, for it indicates that Constable had taken offence at the manner in which da Costa had attempted to persuade him to purchase the *Lapis Crucifer*:

'I am afraid I disgusted you about the *Lapis Crucifer*, I am sure my heart had no notion of your taking it amiss, I sent it to you not only as a curious fossil, but as a fossil of vogue, I concluded you always too sensible to be superstitious, nor did the Idea of superstition ever reach me . . . . .'

The exact nature of Constable's response to the initial offer of the *Lapis Crucifer* is not known, but it seems clear that he, as an educated man of the 'Age of Reason', had resented da Costa's apparent assumption that the status of objects of this sort among less well-informed members of the Roman Catholic Church would in itself make the specimen desirable to him.

The final letter of the ten under consideration is dated 27th January 1761. It is, in part, a response to a letter written by William Constable on 3rd January, in which Constable had evidently been at considerable pains to reassure da Costa of his continuing friendship - despite the acrimonious correspondence of the previous month. Much of the rest of the letter is occupied by a, somewhat philosophical, discussion of what might be termed the different 'modes' of collecting. It ends, however, with an offer by da Costa to supply yet more zoological and botanical material and with an urgent request for monies evidently owed by Constable for specimens already acquired!

It is to be hoped that full transcripts of the letters epitomised above will one day be published; as is - hopefully - already apparent, they represent a minor

treasury of information relating to the character, studies and 'natural knowledge' of William Constable and his sometime mentor and guide, Emanuel Mendes da Costa.

17. Portrait of George Wallis, Gunsmith and antiquary, 1731-1803; watercolour by John Harrison.

CHAPTER SEVEN

WILLIAM CONSTABLE'S ZOOLOGICAL COLLECTION

With the exception of its conchological component, the surviving zoological collection of William Constable is relatively small, and has a decidedly 'miscellaneous' character. The greater part of the surviving collection is still housed at Burton Constable Hall, although thirty-four specimens (including twenty-seven bird and mammal skulls and six marine molluscs) were kindly donated to Hull City Museums by Mr. J.R. Chichester-Constable, in 1966.

In terms of numbers of individual specimens, at least, William Constable's shell collection forms the most notable part of the zoological 'cabinet'. It is currently, however, somewhat disarranged, and further care and study will be necessary before an accurate assessment of its content and significance can be made. One thing that does seem certain is that at least part of Constable's shell collection was acquired from Emanuel Mendes da Costa. Of particular interest in this respect is the presence in the surviving zoological 'cabinet' of a shallow wooden box, or tray, whose interior has been divided, by means of vertical partitions, into a number of compartments, each of which contains numerous small shells. It is just possible that this item is the "large flat Box . . . . curiously partition'd like a Parterre . . . . fill'd with curious small shells" which formed part of the large collection of 'natural curiosities' sent to Constable by da Costa in December, 1760.[109]

Also probably acquired from da Costa were some, if not all, of the tropical corals which survive at Burton Constable Hall; in his letter of 14th August 1760, da Costa notes that he has recently despatched to Burton Constable a collection of corals 'purchased by Mr. Sherwood for William Constable Esq., at the price of ten guineas.'

Preserved specimens are sometimes listed with the live orders. A number of the former survive, bottled or dried, to give a hint as to methods of display in the cabinet. Even a few simple glazed showcases survive. However, a complete example of arrangement can be studied in drawings depicting the cabinet of Bonnier de la Mosson (1702-1744) in Paris - though the latter is wildly extravagant both in design and content.[110]

John Dunn's accounts for dried specimens included 'skeleton of a dragon - £1.4.' in 1764 and 'a dried lizard' that arrived in 1761. Two handsome dried puffer fish have recently been found as have the snakes skin stretched out on matching wooden boards to be suspended from the ceiling, in the manner found in alchemists' laboratories. In March 1763 a London supplier, John Philipson sent £7.9. worth of maritime specimens including a dolphin, sea sparrows, three Venetian vipers and a sea wolfe. Only the cuttle fish and the 'colt' are 'in spirits' so presumably the rest were dried. Also 'in spirits' were the tarantula and scorpion John Dunn noted in 1764 'bring with me'. Today, bottled specimens remaining include a species of *Draco*, the gliding lizard of South-east Asia, and a snake eating a frog.

To obtain stuffed animals Constable sought Thomas Pennant's help. In his notebook (vol.2, rough) he writes 'Inquire of him where I can Acquire a Beautyfull Stuff'd animal. with Eyes teeth. Clawes i.e. completed by Art.' A 'Bird stuff'd - called Pinceau D'Ardenny' came along with other Grand Tour treasures in 1773 sent by James Byres. An unidentified stuffed fish remains on a rather primitive card mount - a method of display also found in the contemporary cabinet at Harvard University. Could this be one of '6 plates Fish --6/- 'sent in 1761?

A number of examples of - presumably - eighteenth century taxidermy do survive including a large Iguana and a very-well-preserved lizard apparently of the genus *Phrynosoma*. Skulls, bones and teeth are well-represented, particularly in that portion of William Constable's zoological collection which is now preserved in the Natural History Department of Hull City Museum.

(Plate 1) Fireplace in the 'Kings bedroom' decorated by Domenico Bartoli; to the designs of T. Lightoler.

(Plate 2) Herbarium sheet; 'Tradescantia Virginian spiderwort, from Constable's own garden, 1745.

49

In 1760 Thomas Knowlton was paid for his designs for a menagerie and in May 1761 its glazing was under discussion. The charming classical building that went up at the north end of the lake, encircled by its own informal garden, must have housed the live purchases that John Dunn sometimes listed in his letters of the 1760's.[111]

For the aviary section John Dunn sent a Virginian nightingale which cost £1.16s, identified as live by the accompanying 'bag and meat.' In 1762 a very expensive purchase was a pair of golden pheasants for eight guineas and a pair of silver 'ditto' for four, plus a bag of wheat. These bird species occur among a long list on a single page catalogue of Joshua Brookes 'zoologist at his Menagery, New Road, Tottenham Court',[112] who sent 2 paris of doves in a cage for £1.5. and in 1776 '3 Best roan ducks' and '4 Large fowles' for nine guineas which were transported to Hull by sea with corn.[113]

One of the accounts for terrestrial creatures indicates there may have been a basin included in the menagerie. In 1764 a frog was bought for 5s. and a pair of turtles for 18s. William James was the supplier of six squirrels that cost £1. which came with a peck of nuts and six dozen of apples, also a cage. A special import were the twenty tortoises sent by James Byres in 1772. Byres however suggested that concerning the nineteen that survived after being kept for three months at Leghorn 'your greenhouse will be a good place for them during Winter if your Gardener will admit them there.'

The menagerie did not outlive Constable, being converted into a house for the estate mason, John Hardy. Thus the former interior arrangements remain unknown.

18. *(above) Goose gun, a seven shot volley weapon with percussion ignition made for Charles Stourton and bearing his crest, a demi-Prior flagellating himself, on the silver escutcheon plate.*

19. *(left) William Constable's invalid chair by Thomas Walker of Hull, one of two surviving wheelchairs; an active traveller and sportsman Constable became a martyr to gout.*

(Plate 3) Rei puta, a whale tooth neck ornament. Now in the Hancock Museum, Newcastle, it is from the former Allan Museum which in turn derived from Marmaduke Tunstall's museum at Wycliffe. (Hancock Museum, University of Newcastle-on-Tyne).

(Plate 4) Candelabrum by Thomas Ward, one of a pair c.1860, in carved giltwood and plaster, nearly eleven feet high until recently stood in the staircase hall at Burton Constable. (Courtesy of Messrs. Sotheby's).

(Plate 5) Palm tree corner stand by Thomas Brooks of Hull.

(Plate 6) The 'dragon chair', a virtuoso piece by Thomas Wilkinson Wallis, carved soon after completing his apprenticeship with Thomas Ward of Hull.

CHAPTER EIGHT

THE GUN CABINET AND THE WALLIS WORKSHOP

William Constable assembled one of the finest gentleman's gun cabinets of the eighteenth century which remained intact for the best part of two hundred years until 1952 when the contents were dispersed in the London sale rooms. Some twenty eight items can be identified as having come from Burton Constable and the late W. Keith Neal was able to bring eighteen of these together in his own remarkable collection.[114] The purchase, repair and maintenance of many of these weapons can be traced through surviving documents although the descriptions are not always sufficient to exactly match a particular piece with its original bill.[115] One of the earliest acquisitions was a truly remarkable gun signed by Simpson of York (see back cover). This seems to be the William Simpson who is recorded in that town 1738-56 as both a gunmaker and a silversmith. The barrel and lockplate are enriched by chiselled decoration and the stock with silver wire inlay, all in the rococo manner while the figure of Britannia on the butt can be related to a similar feature on a scagliola table top by Bartoli still preserved at Burton Constable. Technically the gun is unusual in the replacement of conventional slotted screws by those cut with a square tapering hole for the reception of a turn-key, just like the now familiar Alan Key arrangement. In addition there is a very effective safety mechanism brought into operation by the insertion of a two-pronged tool into a spindle situated just forward of the cock. When the spindle is turned it moves a ratchet on the inside of the lock which moves a steel bolt the end of which comes through the lock plate in front of the frizzle which is thereby firmly locked in the closed position. No other weapon bearing Simpson's name has been recorded and W. Keith Neal suggested that it was made by the London gunsmith Turvey and only decorated by Simpson. Wilson on the other hand compares the gun with a group of fine quality firearms made by Henry Hadley and Benjamin Griffin also of London,

which exhibit comparable silver inlay work and the use of a square-shanked turn-key.[116]

Constable certainly made purchases from Turvey and also James Barbar in the period 1750-8 during which time he was also dealing with the Hull gunsmith Benjamin Burgess. The latter supplied at least one complete gun though he was mainly involved in the supply of powder, and shot, and the repair and cleaning of the weapons kept at the hall. From 1743 Burgess also had a regular job refurbishing the civic armoury. He was to 'new mount and stock and put new locks on the guns' for which he received 17s 6d each but was expected to clean any swords without payment![117] Up until 1773 tasks undertaken for the city fathers included grinding knives and cleaning and mending the gold and silver maces.[118]

Burgess is the only gunsmith known to have been active in Hull during the first half of the eighteenth century but his employment at Burton Constable ceased in October 1759 and his place was taken by George Wallis.[119] The latter was born in Lockington, East Yorks, on April 1731, the son of John Wallis the local blacksmith, and his earliest known work for the Squire is recorded on a bill dated 1 February 1760 'for stocking a large gun' and providing a new lock and brass furniture at a total cost of £1.9s.6d. No documentation of Wallis' apprenticeship has been discovered but we can reasonably surmise that he had learned his trade under the tutelage of Burgess and had come to the attention of Squire Constable while working at the hall on behalf of his master.

Wallis established himself as a craftsman of some note and surviving examples of his work show that he was not only familiar with the latest developments in English gunmaking but was also aware of unusual gun designs of continental origin. He produced (c.1776) a series of light and elegant small-bore airguns, both smoothbore and rifled in which the power was provided by applying a hand-pump to a ball reservoir which was then screwed to the stock. The bar-lock mechanism which these weapons employed was originally devised in Germany or the Low Countries. A very handsome brass-barelled blunderbuss pistol with folding bayonet, now in the Hull Museum, is based on the 1781 patent of John Waters of Birmingham. This piece also shows Wallis utilising locally available materials since the ram-rod, instead of the usual cane or wood, is made from whale-bone (baleen) a product of the Greenland whale fishery, a major Hull enterprise.

There were two other craftsmen working in the city contemporaneously with Wallis namely Richard and William Bottomley (d.1809) who are specifically recorded as gunmakers but neither of them are known to have had any contact with Burton Constable. A delightful pocket pistol with silver wire inlay in the butt signed Sinkler was evidently made by George Sinkler described in the trade directories as an ironmonger and a partner in the firm of Sinkler and Bell, smiths.[120] He is known to have supplied the house with a hearth brush, two locks and a pair of steel snuffers in 1759 and the pistol was certainly made for a discerning client though it is not perhaps of the very highest quality demanded by such as Squire Constable.

Despite the excellence of the work executed by George Wallis and later by his sons only one product of their workshop is known to have been acquired by Squire Constable. Now a part of the W. Keith Neal collection it is an example of a pump-up airgun (though not of the bar-lock type) which bears the Constable crest. Disappointingly there is no surviving record of its purchase or precisely when it was made. The London craftsmen however received a succession of orders for fine guns and pistols, James Barbar being particularly well patronised, as well as Robert Wogdon, William Bailes, James Lowe and Griffin and Tow. This predilection for London-made pieces despite the evident quality of many provincial makers was largely the result of fashion. The London season each year brought the great land owners down from their country seats who then vied with one another in the acquisition of expensive and beautiful works of art, including fine weapons. The potential of such a gathering of gentlemen with long purses encouraged craftsmen to invest in a large stock for display, ready to catch a client's eye, to an extent beyond the means of their provincial 'cousins'.

The Wallis workshop had to be content with regular orders for routine repairs and maintenance and the supply of accessories and miscellaneous shooting requisites such as powder, shot and flints.

In addition its services were called upon to undertake an amazing variety of jobs such as mending a fishing rod (1769), and making repairs to a silver butter boat, (1786) and stove grate (1794) and a theodolite. In 1774 Wallis had also supplied a speaking trumpet to Burton Constable.

On 17th April 1803 George Wallis died aged 73 and was succeeded by his sons George and John who inherited their fathers workshop in Mytongate along with the tools, stock-in-trade and the museum (see below)[121] Francis Constable the new Squire continued to place regular orders for shooting supplies, repairs to be undertaken and spare parts provided. There are also unexpected items like repairing the rigging of a ship model and preparing a box for it.

An unusual fowling piece with a weatherproof lock is unique in being the only weapon known to bear the joint signature of both the brothers but John died at the early age of 34 on 27 June 1811 leaving his elder brother to carry on the business. Over the last decade a considerable number of products of the Wallis workshop have come to light, usually the identity of the original owner is unknown but an exception is a magnificently crafted volley-gun. This rifled goose gun which discharges it seven barrels simultaneously bears the crest of Charles Stourton, a Catholic kinsman of Francis Constable. Later known as Charles Langdale and resident at Houghton Hall, E. Yorks, he was one of the first of his faith to take a seat in parliament, as member for Beverley 1832-4, after the passing of the Relief Acts.[122]

Wallis Jnr. was also appointed supplier of belts, belt plates, swords and accoutrements to the East Riding

*(Plate 7) Self portrait of Thomas Wilkinson Wallis
(1821-1903); signed and dated 1899.
(Town Docks Museum).*

*(Plate 8) Chairs by Thomas Brooks of Hull;
spiral balusters to backs supporting
dragons and crowns.*

(Plate 9) Ebony jardinière from the Richardson workshop.

(Plate 10) Pole screen by Richardson of Hull.

militia and presumably supplied and refurbished guns for them too. In about 1815 he perfected a harpoon gun, the first reliable instrument of its type to be produced for the whaling trade. The ignition was supplied by two massive flintlocks flanking the breech and enclosed withn two metal boxes, provided with hinged flaps, to protect them from salt spray. Supplied at 25 guineas each with six harpoons for nine guineas extra and capable of shooting a line up to a distance of about forty yards, they were recommended by William Scoresby the Whitby whaling captain, in his book entitled *An Account of the Arctic Regions*, published in 1820.

One may note that Wallis had a family connection with the whaling trade through his nephew Richard Wallis Humphreys. Sometime master of the whaleship *Isabella* it was Humphreys who rescued Sir John Ross and his exploration crew after they had been marooned in the Arctic for four years.

When Wallis died in 1833 aged 63 the bulk of his estate passed to Capt. Humphreys who used some of his newly acquired wealth to purchase a schooner which he named *George Wallis* in honour of his uncle. Gunmaking continued on the Mytongate premises however under the management of Edward Humphreys, his brother, and John Crosby Brown their brother-in-law. Edward himself died in 1837 but business carried on in the hands of J.C. Brown who maintained the now traditional contacts with Burton Constable.[123] A brief inventory of arms to be cleaned is signed and dated by him, 4 April 1838 and lists the following '14 dress swords, 12 single guns, 8 brace pistols, 2 stilettoes, 2 Turkish beheading knives, 2 Venetian knives, 11 Sundry daggers, battle axe, air gun, pump and key'.[124] The nature of the weapons give ample evidence of the collecting of exotic items on the Grand Tour while the airgun is almost certainly the example made by Wallis. The latest traceable bill or receipt from Mytongate is dated 29 March 1843 and the workshop finally ceased trading with the death of J.C. Brown aged 42 on 15 June, 1845.

Though the Squire had continued to patronise the successors of George Wallis he also purchased powder shot and other supplies from Samuel Mozeen[125] who had set up in business on his own account shortly before Wallis Jnr. died. Mozeen who had been apprenticed to Wallis and served with him for eighteen years also appears as a witness to his will. Initially Mozeen occupied premises at Mytongate not far from his former employer but moved to Silver Street in 1835. From 1834 he regularly supplied Sir Thomas Constable with goods and services with an accumulated value of £170 at his retirement in 1849.

This severed the last identifiable connection between the gunmaking traditions of the Wallis workshop and Burton Constable, which can be traced from 1760 for a period of nearly one hundred years.

The Silver street premises were taken over by William Needler who is described on his trade card as 'from London'. He was actually the son of a publican, born in 1820 at Pocklington, and the likelihood is that he was apprenticed in Hull and then worked as a journeyman in London, gaining valuable experience in the metropolis, before returning north to set up on his own.[126] Needler established a thriving business selling harpoon guns and a full range of rifles and pistols. A cased set of two pairs of double barrelled pistols bearing what is probably the crest of the Ellerker family, is preserved in the Hull Museum. The quality of his work is confirmed by this continuation of Mozeen's association with Burton Constable a connection which certainly lasted until 1869 but after this time the series of bills and receipts are imperfectly preserved.

After the middle of the nineteenth century the Hull gunsmiths like their counterparts elsewhere in the country were less and less involved in true gunmaking or even assembly and finishing. Most of their stock consisted of Birmingham pieces which they retailed signed with their own names. They would mostly be skilled enough to do repairs and conversions but by the end of the century the typical gunsmith was a retailer pure and simple. Most general stock came from the highly developed Birmingham gun trade and only a handful of, mainly London-based, gunsmiths continued to provide hand-built weapons to order. Some established names are still in evidence notable Holland and Holland and Purdey who specialise in shotguns and rifles made to order.

20. *A contemporary illustration of Richard Greene's (1716-93) museum at Lichfield; note the South Sea artefacts on the left, gun cabinet on the right, and shells and miscellaneous curiosities at the rear. This gives some impression of the arrangement of the eighteenth century museum.*

(Plate 11) Parisian fall-front bureau;
modified by Richardson's.

(Plate 12) All gold chair with tapestry seat,
by Richardson's of Hull.

CHAPTER NINE

THE WALLIS MUSEUM, ITS INSPIRATION AND CONTEMPORARIES

During the second half of the eighteenth century probably every gentleman who had embarked on the Grand Tour purchased not only paintings and sculptures but a miscellaneous collection of curiosities, medals, seals and intaglios. There was also an increasing tendency for these gentlemen to indulge a fashion for the natural sciences and gather together *natural curiosities* including shells, fossils, minerals as well as animal and botanical specimens. A number of individuals created something more substantial than the typical country house cabinet and one of the greatest private museums was created by Sir Ashton Lever Bt.[127] Originally housed at Alkrington Hall, his seat near Manchester, it was eventually opened to the public at Leicester House in London where it included a special display of the native artefacts brought back from Cooks third expedition by J.R. Forster. The enthusiasm for making museums was not however confined to the gentry and aristocracy and Richard Greene (1716-93), apothecary, of Lichfield, a kinsman of Samuel Johnson, is another seminal figure in the origins of the modern museum.[128] These collections were open to the public and though a charge was usually made this was an attempt to cover expenses or restrict the flow of visitors rather than to make a profit. In Lever's case this was to be a forlorn hope and the *Holophusicon*, as he grandly called his enormous assemblage of material, proved such a strain on his purse it had to be sold by public lottery. William Bullock,[129] a silversmith by training, on the other hand took a wholeheartedly entrepreneurial approach to his collection which was widely toured around the country before being displayed in London at the Egyptian Hall. The latter's exotic facade was all part of his salesmanship and Bullock's museum was a key element in the history of public entertainments.

Wallis, born in the small village of Lockington, near Driffield, set himself up in business in 1760 by which time he was twenty-nine years of age. He is unlikely to

have found much time for travelling and his horizons would largely be confined to the county of Yorkshire and the contacts made through his craft as a gunsmith. The cabinets of Squire Constable and other local gentlemen would no doubt have attracted his attention and these and the exotica brought into the port of Hull by sea captains and arctic whalers would all have been a stimulus to Wallis and sources in the formation of his own museum.

The following notice appeared in the very first issue of the *Hull Advertiser*, Saturday 5 July, 1794:

**Wallis's collection
of Natural and Artificial Curiosities**

Consisting of Medals, Coins, Ores, Petrefactions, etc., with a very curious assortment of Firearms, Swords and Daggers.

'The Proprietor, however unwilling he may be to deprive the Public (more especially his friends and customers) of the pleasure they have so long expressed in contemplating the works of Art and Nature, at length finds himself under an unavoidable necessity of laying a restraint on the indiscriminate resort of spectators, daily increasing, to the great interruption of his time and prejudice of his business. He therefore takes this method to signify that his MUSEUM will be open for the inspection of the curious, every day (Sundays excepted) between the hours of ten and one in the forenoon, and two and five in the afternoon, at ONE SHILLING each person when due attendance will be given.'

The earliest reference to the museum is inserted in a description of the Hull whaling industry for the year 1788 published in Hadley's *History of Hull*.[130] Evidently it was the curiosities of natural history which took the chronicler's eye though there must already have been a considerable quantity of antique weapons on display:

'The sword of the Xiphias,[131] the horn of the Unicorn,[132] and the head of the Sea-horse,[133] are all in the collection of that ingenious artist Mr. George Wallis of Myton Street; a collection which if displayed with the advantage of a convenient repository, and dignified with the patronage of an illustrious proprietor, would justly engage the attention of the most celebrated virtuosi of the age, on account of the rare articles of which it consists. In the accummulation of which Mr. Wallis' genuine attachment to, and due administration of the works of nature, and improvements of art (void of the vain pride of possessing what is difficult to be obtained) are as conspicuous as his polite assiduity in the exhibition of them to all degrees of persons, who hint their desires to be indulged in that account.'

A more extensive description of the museum is given in John Tickell's *History of Hull* published in 1798.[134] It is particularly valuable because it records some of the outstanding examples of antique weapons which had been acquired: 'In this street (i.e. Myton Street or Mytongate) lived the ingenious Mr. George Wallis, gunsmith, who with incredible industry, and at a charge seemingly much above his ability, has made a choice and valuable collection of curiosities, both natural and artificial, amongst which are a large collection of guns, of every description, from the first invention of these destructive weapons to the present time; curious pistols, and a great variety of different sorts of warlike instruments, as swords, spears, daggers, etc. particularly one of the last brought from the East Indies, said to have belonged to the great Tamerlane. A sword by Edward the Black Prince, with a large black pommel, and on its blade this inscription 'Edwardus Prins Angliae' and another from Henry the VIII inlaid with gold,[135] and made after he had taken the town of Boulogne, as appears from the description on its blade, alluding to that event; a large assortment of ancient spurs, amongst which is one that General Fairfax wore at the Battle of Naseby, and another which belonged to Ferdinand Leigh, a colonel in the army of King Charles I, the rowel of which forms a star set in a birds eye, having a dozen points, three inches and a half from the head; the whole curiously wrought and gilt. A curious collection of ancient and modern medals, struck in gold, silver and copper; shells, minerals and a great variety of other varieties well worth the attention of the curious.'

Though some of the historical associations may be speculative the attribution of the decorated sword to Henry 8 has been confirmed by modern research. The blade of the weapon, described in the Royal inventories as a 'wood knife' is engraved with scenes of the siege of Boulogne, 1544, by the Spanish swordsmith and damascener Diego de Caias. It was one of the King's personal arms and after passing through a number of collections at home and abroad, now reposes once again in the possession of the royal family at Windsor Castle. This and many other items were very probably obtained by Wallis from clients amongst the local gentry yet others by exchange with fellow proprietors of museums. In the 1782 catalogue of Richard Greene's famous establishment at Lichfield, Staffs., is the following entry:

'An airgun, on the newest construciton, made by the truly ingenious and worthy Mr. Wallis of Hull, who presented it to the museum'.[136]

On the other side of the Pennines, in Manchester, lived another and now largely forgotten antiquary by the name of Thomas Baritt.[137] He was well known among his contemporaries and it would be remarkable indeed considering their common interest in armour and weapons if he and Wallis had never met or corresponded. No direct evidence of such a contact exists but both were in touch with Greene, to whom Barrit gave two models of medieval tombs and refers to in his papers as 'My Worthy friend Mr. Green, apothecary.'

A saddler by trade Barritt had only one leg, a deficiency made up for with a cork substitute. He claimed descent from good yeoman stock in Derbyshire and his genealogical studies and notes on antiquities can still be read with interest. Some indication of Barritt's standing amongst his fellow antiquarians and *literati* is indicated by his election to membership of the Literary and Philosophical Society of Manchester in 1776, only five years after its foundation. In a manuscript[138] record of his collection of arms and armour illustrated by his own splendid watercolour drawings he shows a sword which he imagined had belonged to the Black Prince. Modern scholars recognise it as one of a group of hangers or *couteaux de chasse* of seventeenth century date thought to have been assembled in England though the blades are apparently of German manufacture. Each is inscribed EDWARDUS PRINS ANGLIE and usually struck with the running wolf mark associated with the sword cutlers of Passau and Solingen. Barritt's example had belonged some eighty years previously to the park-keeper of Garswood, near Wigan, Lancs, home of the Gerard family. The grip is of staghorn with each arm of the short crossguard terminating in a hemispherical finial while the pommel is roughly tea-cosy shaped with a scroll-like adjuct at one side. He mentions a similar sword then at Armathwaite Castle, Cumberland, said to have been left behind by Edward I in 1306 when he made his headquarters at nearby Lanercost. The latter is the weapon referred to by Tickell which had passed into the Wallis museum at Hull and is now in the Tower Armouries, London. It chiefly differs from Barrit's sword by having a basket hilt.[139]

George Wallis died in 1803 and he was of sufficient celebrity that a subscription was raised to publish an engraved portrait. Based on a watercolour drawing by John Harrison the mezzotint was executed by John Raphael Smith (engraver to the Prince of Wales) under the patronage of the Duke of Clarence, the future William 4. Wallis is depicted holding in his hands a wheellock pistol, one of a group made in 1579 for Julius, Duke of Brunswick-Lüneberg; it is probably the pistol now in the Victoria and Albert Museum (inv.no.M638.1927) acquired from Major V. Farquharson in 1955.[140]

Richard Greene had died in 1793 and seven yars later the arms and armour from the Lichfield museum was sold for 150 guineas to William Bullock, proprietor of the Liverpool Museum. His first collection is said to have been established in 1795 at Sheffield but he subsequently moved to an address in Church Street, Liverpool. The title page of *A companion to the Liverpool Museum* (5th edition, 1807) describes him as jeweller and silversmith to HRH the Duke of Gloucester. No trace of the Wallis airgun presented to Greene can be discovered in this or any of the subsequent editions of the catalogue but the list of benefactors indicates that several of the Wallis family contributed to the material on display. What the particular item each gave is not specified but the museum included a large variety of natural history specimens and curiosities in addition to the armour and weapons.

In September 1800 *Mrs*.Bullocks grand cabinet of wax figures was exhibited at the *Ship* tavern.[141] These full size effigies of members of the royal family, Nelson, Dr. Franklin, Tippoo Sultan and many other historical personages proved such a success that they remained on view in Hull until the end of the year. A few years later Bullocks museum, or rather a sample of more than three hundred articles arrived in the city and a contemporary handbill announces:

'Exhibition.

Just arrived, and to be seen in that commodious house, in Scale Lane, occupied by the late Dr. Darling. Bullocks celebrated cabinet of curiosities, etc'.[142]

Dr. Darling is one of a number of contributors resident in Hull whose names appear in the list of benefactors recorded in the catalogue. The material exhibited included a cabinet of wax figures 'as large as life', a collection of busts of famous people modelled in rice paste, a model ship of glass, a small Egyptian mummy, a quantity of 'ancient arms and armour', and native artefacts from China, America and the South Seas. This temporary venue in Scale Lane was only a few minutes walk from the Wallis museum and clearly afforded plenty of opportunity for the purchase or exchange of antiquities between the two establishments.

Then in September 1807 the *whole* of Bullocks collected was transported across the Pennines to Hull and displayed at 8 Market Place where upwards of four thousand items were arranged in a series of five apartments.[143] Admission was two shillings each, a perpetual ticket cost 10s.6d, and a catalogue a further two shillings. By the end of October the price of entry had been reduced to a shilling and the last week in November seems to have been the final opportunity to see the museum before it was packed up again for a journey south.[144] Surviving copies of the catalogue indicate that the sixth edition, dated 1808, was printed by J. Ferraby of Hull.

Subsequently Bullock moved to Bath and then to London and the twelfth edition of the catalogue published in 1812, now entitled *A Companion to Mr. Bullocks Museum and Pantherion* still credits Mr. Wallis and George Wallis though of course Wallis Snr. was dead by this time.[145] The 1813 and 1814 issues refer only to Mr. Wallis, that is to say the younger Wallis who maintained and increased the Mytongate museum after his father's death. Unfortunately there is no inventory of the collections in Hull prior to a printed catalogue produced in 1833 soon after the death of Wallis Jnr.[146] Although the gunmaking business continued in the hands of Edward Humphreys and J.C. Brown it was decided to sell off the museum and the catalogue which is divided into over a thousand lots was evidently drawn up with the intention of having a public auction. There is no evidence that this ever took place and the contents were in fact sold piecemeal over the next ten to fifteen years. The latest reference in the local guidebooks appears in 1836 when the editor expresses the hope that 'this curious and valuable assemblage of articles of vertu now on sale will be purchased entire as dispersion into many hands would seriously deteriorate its value'.[147] Perhaps the strangest circumstance is the apparent lack of interest by the Hull Literary and Philosophical Society.[148] Founded in 1822 the following year they decided to establish a museum of their own and quickly acquired collections of geological and natural history specimens. Numbers of ethnographic items were also added to the store of treasures including a shrunken head from New Zealand, two Eskimo Kayaks and some Arctic birds donated by Sir John Ross as well as the usual miscellany of oddities and *lusus naturae*.

Many of Wallis's finest guns and weapons were still owned by Mrs. Humphreys and John Crosby Brown in 1842. The former had possession of the sword of Henry 8 for example and the latter the sword from Armathwaite Castle. Subsequently most of the best pieces were purchased by Lord Londesborough and taken to his seat at Grimston Park, near Tadcaster.[149]

The source of most of the contents of the Wallis museum is unknown but the 1833 catalogue does include the names of a handful of the original donors and benefactors. A double-barrelled fowling piece by Boutet of Versailles[150] once the property of Napoleon was presented by Col. Thomas Thornton, a notable shot and responsible for reviving an interest in the ancient sport of falconry. A double-barrelled rifle by De Saintes of Versailles,[151] the barrels inlaid with gold, was presented by General Ralph Burton whose life it had been the means of preserving; 'He was out shooting alone while in America, when immediately after killing a bird, an Indian who had been lying in ambush rushed towards him. The general with his remaining barrel fired and shot him, and took from him a scalping knife, a scalp and a tomahawk, all of which are preserved in this museum'.[152] Other donors were James Brown Esq. of Hull, Dr. Trebor, General Lennox, Capt. O'Hara RN, Joseph Sykes, (a Hull merchant) and Capt. John McBride. The latter was in command of the *Artois* which in 1781 captured two Dutch privateers; a French swivel gun captured by McBride is now at Warwick Castle.

Relatively few items can be traced down to the present though we have noted the sword of Henry 8, the Armathwaite sword and the sixteenth century wheellock all of which have found a resting place in the national collections. Another edged weapon, the sword of state of Nicholas da Ponte, Doge of Venice (1578-83) passed to Beriah Botfield and was part of a collection formed at Norton Hall, c.1840-50 purchased in 1942 by the Tower Armouries, London.[153] One curious sword which cannot now be discovered is the minature weapon presented by Count Joseph Boruwlaski, the Polish dwarf. Originally given to him by the Duchess of Devonshire it may be the one depicted in the portrait owned by the Royal College of Surgeons.[154] Boruwlaski visited Hull in May, 1803, to give a concert and stayed at an address in Finkle Street, just round the corner from the Wallis museum in Mytongate.[155]

Also listed in the 1833 catalogue were a number of artefacts from Tahiti which very likely came from one of the South Sea expeditions of Capt. Cook. Richard Greene had a quantity of material from the third voyage

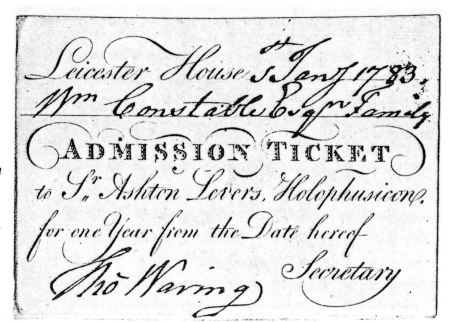

21. William Constable's ticket for Sir Ashton Lever's Holophusicon in Leicester Square, London.

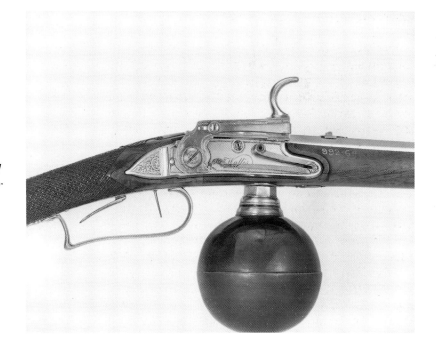

22. Airgun by George Wallis Snr., c.1776; a light, elegantly constructed piece with a pump-up globe reservoir and bar-lock mechanism.

donated by Sir Ashton Lever (1729-88) of Alkrington Hall, Manchester. The latter had been given the opportunity of acquiring this material through the influence of Daines Barrington, lawyer and antiquary, who thought Lever a much more suitable recipient than the British Museum! Lever's museum was initially displayed at his country seat but in 1774 the Leverian museum or *Holophusicon* opened its doors at Leicester House in London. Sold by lottery in 1786 this vast accummulation was dispersed by auction in 1809. Amongst the buyers was William Bullock but purchases were also made by Sir John Soane, Lord Stanley and for the Hunterian Museum and the Royal College of Surgeons. The material brought to England by Cook is therefore difficult to provenance because of this complicated circulation through a number of inter-related collections which were formed and dispersed during the late eighteenth and early nineteenth centuries. Tunstall established his own museum at his London town house in Welbeck Street and William Constable while in the capital lived only a short distance away in Mansfield Street where he also established a museum.[156] Tunstall's collections were moved to his country estate at Wycliffe in 1780-1 (or 1782, see note 31) and were bequeathed to William Constable along with a considerable inheritance of land and property when Marmaduke died, 11 October 1790, in his forty-eighth year. Constable survived him by a mere six months and the museum at Wycliffe was offered for sale by Edward Sheldon his nephew and heir. On the 14th and 15th May 1792 at Mr. Christies auction room in Pall Mall a large number of natural history specimens, antiquities and art objects came under the hammer. These are listed in *'A catalogue of the genuine museum of natural and artificial curiosities of William Constable Esq., late of Yorkshire, dec., chiefly collected by the late Marmaduke Tunstall Esq. comprising an extensive variety of shells, corals, minerals, insects and other curious subjects of a natural history, antiquities, carvings in ivory, oriental works of art, bronzes, magnificent mahogany cabinets with glazed drawers, superb performances in shell work, a patent electrifying machine by Nairne etc'.*[157] These seem to have been items regarded as duplicates or of secondary interest from both Constable and Tunstalls acquisitions. The core of the material from Wycliffe[158] was purchased from Edward Sheldon by George Allan[159] for £700 and transferred to his home at Blackwell Grange, Darlington, where it was opened to public view in June 1792. Augmented and improved during the remaining years of his life the collections ultimately formed the basis of the Hancock Museum in Newcastle where many relics of Cooks voyages can still be seen.[160] (pl.3)

Allan compiled a manuscript catalogue of the Wycliffe collection as it was when he acquired it. Sadly this is now missing but he described 'a large collection of curiosities brought by Capt. Cook from Otaheite etc'. According to Fox[161] there were also catalogues from the museums of Daniel Boulter[162], George Humphreys[163] and Sir Ashton Lever marked to indicate articles purchased from their collections by Allan.

All of these contained material from Cooks expeditions, Lever's chiefly if not entirely from the third expedition and George Humphreys probably from both the first and second voyages The *rei puta* a carved and decorated sperm tooth neck decoration which is in the Hancock Museum appears in the portrait of a Maori drawn by Sydney Parkinson in 1770 during the first voyage. Some at least of the South Sea material may have been given to William Constable, or swapped for other material, by his half-brother. Constables interest in all kinds of artificial and natural curiosities is not in doubt and still surviving in the Burton Constable archive is a ticket to the 'Holophusicon' for him and his 'family' giving admission for a whole year beginning 1 January 1783. It was intended that Marmaduke Tunstall was to be one of the chief recipients of the collections from the third voyage along with Sir Ashton Lever, Sir Joseph Banks, the British Museum and an unidentified R.S. possible Richard Salisbury (1761-1829), botanist and fellow of the Royal Society. Since there is no catalogue of the items originally at Welbeck Street it is now impossible to say which items now in the Hancock Museum were acquired directly by Tunstall or were added later. It is clear however that the provenance of the

South Sea material is from the Cook expeditions.[164]

It has been noted that the Wallis museum contained ethnographic material which included items from Tahiti. These were very probably original specimens collected during Cook's expedition and in the natural history section were 'parts of (sea) lion and seal skin, said to have been killed by Capt. Cook.'[165] These Soth Sea relics may have come from Constable or from Tunstall but given the wide-ranging movements of local ships might have been given to either Wallis the father or son by some seafaring customer or acquaintance. It may be noted that there was a local connection with Capt. Cook in as much as William Hammond (1729-93), sometime chairman of the Hull Dock Co. was responsible for arranging the sale of the two Whitby vessels to the Admiralty which became the *Resolution* and *Adventure* for his second voyage 1772-5. Hammond was also founder of the Hull Trinity House Navigation School and it is worth noting, as a possible source of inspiration for the Wallis museum, that the Trinity House itself has its own remarkable collection which is still extant.[166] The oldest collection of antiquities in the city it contains material from all over the world donated by the seafaring brethren including fine ship models, weapons, paintings, relics of the whaling industry, ethnographical specimens and curiosities. Perhaps the most striking is the Greenland Kayak, complete with the figure of an Eskimo dressed in a sealskin jacket; it was deposited in 1613 by Andrew Barker of the *Heartsease*.

23. 'Wood-knife' of Henry 8, decorated with damascene work illustrating the siege of Bolougne in 1544 by the Spanish swordsmith Diego de Caias. It once formed part of the Wallis Museum.
(Reproduced by gracious permission of Her Majesty the Queen).

CHAPTER TEN

CONSTABLE THE IMPROVER - THE CREATION OF A LANDSCAPE GARDEN

In 1784 Constable wrote to his brother, Marmaduke concerning the state of his park 40 years ago. He described a 'wilderness' with swamps, 'gorse and whin higher than a man on horseback' and 'deep ridge and furrow...' but he continued 'Now all is removed and at great Expence'.[167]

After a decade of apparent indecision Constable began to tackle his 'improvements' in the mid 1750's by creating flower, vegetable and botanic gardens near the house, a task he was aided in by Thomas Knowlton, Lord Burlington's gardener at Londesborough.[168]

By 1767 he had finally decided to employ 'Capability' Brown to transform the 'wilderness' into a landscaped park.[169] The pattern of the old park is delineated in a small scale pencil plan ascribed by Constable to Brown, dated 1767. It shows the formal avenues radiating east, west, south and south west from the house and a chain of fish ponds on the site of today's lakes, all features depicted in the late 17th century portrait of the house and grounds still in the Great Hall. Thomas White, Timothy Lightoler and Brown had all submitted landscape plans though of a varying extent. White's large scale water coloured survey and proposals were modestly charged at 10 guineas and as Deborah Turnbull suggested to me, may well have been of assistance to Brown. Lightoler's rococo designs show landscaping for the area round the new stable block and there is also his plan for the new kitchen gardens.[170] Brown's rejected small pencil design of 1767 recently discovered is really rococo with its elliptical shapings of trees and water encircling the grounds. It is similar to his design for Combe Park near Coventry (1778), where there is an equally flat topography and to Shenstone's Leasowes nearby. Of Brown's executed work some detailed drawings and sketches survive at the house.

The lawns

Between 1769 and 1782, Brown attended Constable at least 9 times.[171] For his meeting in 1769, Constable's preliminary notes survive in a commonplace notebook commencing 'Mr. Brown, how to clump my avenues... ...' For subsequent meetings, from 1772, it was the estate steward Robert Raines who minuted the annual site visits. These 'Hints and directions by Mr. Brown' along with Brown's 1767 small scale survey and the rejected plan have recently been discovered at Burton Constable by Mr. Matthews of Cobham Land Use Consultants. The documents reveal Constable and Brown in the dual roles of "improvers" and creators of "neatness and beauty" to quote Constable's own words. First and foremost the drainage of the swampy areas was facilitated by trenching prior to tree planting,[172] as well as in the enlargement of the existing fishponds into two lakes. Brown preferred his clumps of trees to be large, calling any others "pimples on the face of nature". Such clumps and the shelter belt planting, served commercial as well as aesthetic purposes. Brown gave careful instructions for the "promiscuous" planting and also the thinning and general maintenance of his plantations.

A year after Constable had returned from the Grand Tour in 1772, the appointment of a new overseer of the landscaping, James Clark, at £50 per annum, signalled the commencement of the new work - which began on the lawns near the house. From 1771 a stove garden was being created near the menagerie so that the old one could be removed from West Lawn. Near the house, the south western, diagonal avenue (Roehill Avenue) was to be removed. The West Lawn was then clear for staking out ready for tree planting, a job that Brown himself usually seems to have performed.

The design shown on Brown's detailed drawing of the Lawn and stable areas was completed by 1779. The trees were planted so as to frame the house to north and south, leaving an open prospect to the west theoretically giving uninterrupted views toward and from the lake. The sheep grazed lawn was to be carefully levelled where in sight from the house, and was to be encircled by a new Ha Ha continuing the sweep of the old moat. The Lawn was to be drained into the Ha Ha. The East Lawn was to be similarly staked and planted, after a total and permanent removal of the East Avenue, but here the clumps were planted theatrically to reveal and conceal the mansion, thus adding a little drama for the travellers along the newly aligned Marton road.

Elsewhere Constable's intentions concerning clumping were only partially carried out. Brown and his patron agreed to retain most of South and West (or menagerie) Avenue. Roe Hill Avenue was kept wholly intact only beyond the lake, thus improving the vista toward the lake from the house.

Work on transforming the fish ponds began in 1775, the workmen being paid between 2d and 5d per cubic yard of soil removed, (approximately one ton) according to the difficulty of the excavation. The upper Menagerie lake and the lower 'Long Stanks' were given gently curving banks sloping down to a three foot depth of water. One of the two islands made in Long Stanks was removed. (The island now in Menagerie lake is early 19th century).

The 'Raines' notes indicate that such modifications of the original plan were not unusual, in the correction of unforeseen defects. Of Brown's many sketch ideas, two survive for the lake. The earlier version had an obvious round termination at the Sproatley end but that executed ended in a small inlet surrounded by trees so that it appeared to continue its river-like course. Such illusions were created elsewhere by Brown for example at Wimpole.

In 1778 Hawksworth 'cast' the new drive from Sproatley over Brown's brick and stone bridge, that disguised the dam separating the new upper and lower lakes. From here the house came picturesquely into an oblique view that took in both the water and the new plantations. On the other hand the lake views seen from the house could have been improved, had Brown done as he intended in his first small drawing, or as he attempted to suggest at his meetings - and brought the lake nearer the house.

Brown's decision in the end, to retain some of the avenues as he had done at Chillington and Ingestre is an indication of the special significance he held for mature trees, especially perhaps in such a flat landscape. Poulson describes the two western avenues as of ancient elm and of chestnut respectively, which would have accorded with the policy Brown shared with Constable that native trees were best.

This preference for native trees however is not always borne out by the accounts from the wide range of nurserymen that Constable continued to patronise.[173] Among the first of the new trees to arrive was a large shipment from France to the value of £49.10. that Brown "jardinier du roi" had organised for the spring planting season of 1773. However, soon after, Clark was supplying, from an unknown source, 300 eight foot elms and 94 seven foot limes as well as 30 planes. In 1775 more native trees came from Grimwood of Chelsea who sent 2000 small birch and 300 six-seven foot ones as well as two thousand seedling beech. Brown had suggested that the large shelter belt between West and South avenues be planted with local acorns and beech mast that he would supply. 'Transplanted' alders came in a collection of mostly foreign trees from Telfords of York in 1779 when the lake was nearing completion. There were only 168 alders from Telford soon to be supplemented by 2000 imported from Holland through the agency of two well known Hull business men Thomas Howarth and Isaac Broadley. Their progeny still grace the lake. Also in 1779 Andrew Carr of Cottingham supplied 900 larch trees. Apart from the latter and yew, most conifers came as seed. Now only yews survive and continue to contribute the variation of colour, texture and shape that Brown intended. Among Telfords new introductions were the American species in which Constable had developed a special interest, including the Virginian flowering ash, Carolinian poplars and scarlet oaks. The clumps were probably under-planted with the "loo hollies transplanted 9 & 10 Inches" also sent, while colour counterchange was achieved by the planting of 38 single or double flowering almonds. Two dozen of these had additionally come from Perfects of Pontefract a year earlier. Ornamental interest is also evident in the long list from the Cottingham firm of Phillipson and Scales bill of 1790, which is also notable because up to then, local firms such as Joseph French of Hull and Sigstons of Beverley had been providing mainly seeds or plants for the kitchen garden, including in the case of Sigston's of Beverley, a variety of pineapple plants.[174]

Though the precise siting for the ornamental shrubs and trees is lacking, the 1779 surveys and the evidence on the ground today both indicate that the majority of Brown's intentions regarding tree planting were carried out. However except for the bridge his proposals for buildings in the landscape were not accepted. On Roe Hill he proposed first a temple cum observatory, and then an arch, but neither was built, nor was the 'false bridge' - a favourite contrivance of his, here proposed for the head of the Menagerie lake, for which Brown promised a drawing in 1782. A watercolour sketch for a false bridge and cascade has recently been identifed, complete with William Constable's instructions, as to how to paint the effect of rocks and cascades. The watercolour is competent and may be from Brown's office.

Several of the other architectural features Brown planned have a castellated theme in sympathy with the Tudor pele tower. He might even have designed the castellated engine house near the Sproatley avenue which he directed should be painted stone colour.[175] In 1774 suggested similar treatment for the castellated entrance screen to the domestic offices, which are not unlike one of his designs for Blenheim. Finally it was Wyatt's handsome castellated Sproatley gateway that was made the new entrance to the park. Thomas Atkinson of York's dry house or orangery however broke different ground for both rebuilding and the sculpture adorning it were uncompromisingly classical, a change that followed Brown's death. Both buildings still make important accents in the quiet landscape that did so much to complement neoclassical taste.[176]

The Victorian landscape

William Constable and Brown had clearly been somewhat reluctant to cut down the avenues except the infilling of that to the north. But since no attempt was made to plant within the lines of the south and west avenues, it became a simple matter to carry out any reinstatement and this was achieved during the ownership of Sir Clifford Constable. Where Capability Brown had suggested a Temple or an Arch on Roe Hill, Sir Clifford placed a huge pedestal and statue of a stag, and the west avenue was further embellished with similar pedestals which supported a pair of 'Marly' horses - the originals of which now stand at the foot of the Champs Elysees in Paris. Nearer the house, this reversion to formality also included the creation of a French Garden (noted by Poulson in 1841) whose walks were lined with pyramids or Irish yews alternating with single statues or groups. For the most part, these were copies of well-known Antique statues; some of them were selected from those offered in the catalogue of Matthew Johnson of New Road, now Euston Road, in west London, but the Constables also studied the similar catalogue of Messrs. Austin & Seeley. The surviving sheets of Johnson's catalogue (post marked 1856) include an illustration of a stag which at life size cost £6.0. and a pedestal 7ft 8inches high at £20. Unfortunately Johnson's claim that his product, an artifical stone, was 'warranted to resist frost', has proved false because the iron armature within the figures has rusted, bursting open the arms or legs concerned. In its heyday the French Garden was illuminated by gas lights supplied from the private gas works that Sir Clifford had built to the south of the Riding House.

Next to Lady Marianne's boudoir facing the garden there was added a small richly gilded conservatory cum aviary, probably designed by Henry Lockwood then of Hull. In contrast to Atkinson's Orangery Lockwood added Elizabethan cresting to harmonise with the architecture of the main building. Lockwood's conservatory has been demolished and the garden layout simplified in recent years, a change counterbalanced by the restoration of the nearby Orangery.

24. Heraldic chair, probably by a member of the Highams family, the estate carpenters.

25. Chair with star motif like that found on the bookcases in the long gallery; attributed to William and Thomas Wrightson of Beverley.

CHAPTER ELEVEN

THE LIBRARY

Introduction

The creation of private libraries was of long standing, some, such as those of Sir Thomas Bodley or Sir Hans Sloane, eventually becoming libraries accessible to the public. More often, they were dispersed, either because of the lack of interest of succeeding generations, or because their intrinsic value provided an additional source of capital for those who wished to lead quite different lives. Though the typical Georgian library was the outcome of book collecting, many were to be supplemented by collections of historic manuscripts and engravings. The more cautious collector brought only what he could see; others took risks by subscribing toward new works, not all of which reached publication. The subscription list not only helped the author or his publisher, it announced to the world that the subscribers regarded themselves as men of taste and of a certain standing in society. (Similar subscription lists, typically with the amount subscribed, were also published by charities such as hospitals or for 'public' works such as the Assembly Rooms at York). The vogue for book subscription began in earnest in the early eighteenth century, for example, for Colin Campbell's *Vitruvius Britannicus*, and continued with undiminished vigour until well into the nineteenth century. The family name does not appear in the lists for Campbell's three volumes, but Cuthbert Constable did subscribe for William Kent's *Designs of Inigo Jones* of 1727, and toward Lord Burlington's Assembly Rooms at York. The Constables were not, however, avid subscribers, preferring to buy upon publication, from France and Italy as well as England. The books William Constable did subscribe too indicate his absorbing interest in all forms of natural history and science - for example William Curtis *Flora Londinensis* (1777-89), William Speechley's *A treatise on the culture of pineapples* 1779 and Joseph Priestley on *The history and present discoveries relating to Vision*, 1772.

Constable's industry in reading can be assessed from innumerable extracts in the surviving commonplace notebooks.[177] The latter were in pencil and seem to have been copied into other memo books in ink as the permanent version with occasional personal annotations. This record also reveals his use of authorities ancient or modern in formulation of his own thoughts.

Book storage

Cuthbert and William Constable collected a considerable library, wide ranging in its subject matter and, from c.1742, housed along the walls of Cuthbert's 'Gallery' constructed in the 1730's. Here too, William conducted his scientific experiments, and for both father and son, it was the most significant room in the house. In the south of Cuthbert's gallery, there was a principal bedroom and dressing room, and, after advice from Capability Brown in 1769, these were 'thrown together' to form the present room. This involved the dismantling of the south wall bookcases and their repositioning on the east wall. A second library was formed out of a closet in the shallow south-western bay window. By the 1770's, the whole had become unmanageable, and William set about a radical rearrangement, methodically catalogued, shelved and numbered. By 1775, the number of books had reached nearly 9,600, a figure still quoted in the 1791 inventory, a figure that ignored a further sixteen years of purchasing. Some books, such as those on science, served a practical purpose. Others, such as the series on architecture and Antiquity, were studied prior to embarkation on the Grand Tours, and afterwards used as the basis for new designs for the decoration of the interior. Less than four percent of wholly new works, i.e. for William, published after his father's death, were in the main Gallery, while 35 percent of the latter's purchases were installed in the Gallery Closet. The remainder, in another room called 'Library' were not apparently catalogued in 1775, though they amounted to some 2,600 works. Possibly they were manuscripts.

Book classification

The 1775 catalogue shows that the Long Gallery housed 4679 books, which according to the description in the heirlooms list of 1791, were housed in thirteen bookcases of elm (also oak) with sash doors. Today the bookcases remain unaltered in form or purpose, even displaying the locks and escutcheons made by John Marshall, whitesmith of Beverley in 1742.[178] When the adjacent library closet was added this was also lined with shelves containing in 1775, 2117 volumes while 'the Library' contained 2575 volumes on shelves and 229 manuscripts.

The introduction to the 1775 catalogue lists the sections in the Long Gallery. In A & C are 'Miscellanea', in B, D, E & F are 'Literae Humaniores' including medical works and E, G, H, and I house 'Historia profana' which includes natural philosophy, geography, travel and descriptions of antiquities, while the large section K, L, M, and N is for 'Theologia' also including a good deal of ecclesiastical history. The library closet catalogue contains all these classifications including the majority of Constable's scientific books.

The books are catalogued alphabetically - though sometimes the author and at other times the title is described first. For example the book *Hortus Cliffortianus* occurs in the first column with no indication that the author is Linnaeus. Five other columns indicate; the number of volumes; the town and date of publication; the bookcase letter; the number of pages; and the size *viz* folio, quarto, octavo or duodecimo. A typical entry reads:

Moxon's Mechanical exercises   Lon.1700   D181   8vo

Purchasing customs

Constable employed both London and York booksellers, some of the surviving accounts indicating the manner and scale of his purchases. For example, between November 1768 and 1769 - he spent £124.12s.5d. at Benjamin White,[179] on books concerning both the humanities and natural philosophy and natural history by mainly English and French authors. The latter include Diderot's 'Planche de 'Encyclopedie tom 6' which cost £4.17s.6d., bound, from which Constable extracted copious notes. Some of the volumes included those published by the Aldine Press in Venice, and included works printed in vellum, another was printed at Horace Walpole's private press at Strawberry Hill. Like many other bibliophiles, Constable liked to buy works unbound so that they could be bound up to his own specification, and there are numerous bills from firms such as Todd & Sotheran of York (now in London), itemising books bound to special order.

One of the few works remaining unbound and in its original paper wrappers is Robert & James Adam's *Works in Architecture* that appeared in parts in the 1770's. His particular set is the one in which the subscriber paid extra to have a selection of plates hand coloured. Many volumes arrived unbound but 'sewed, for example, 'on may 22nd *Phil.tran.vol 57 sewed*' cost 15s.6d. In the case of 7 volumes of *Oeuvres de Voltaires* in quarto, the cost of binding is separately noted and added £1.15s to the cost (£5). It seems that plates also had to be added by the bookseller at times for White charged 6s. for 'the Plates to Buffon's *Hist. Naturelle*' Tom 3 & 4' and then 6s. for 'putting them into the volume.'

The accounts from John Todd too are preserved, sometimes describing the binding whether morocco, calf or boards or with gilt edges. For example in 1785 Todds charged 1s.9d. for an octavo volume of '*Priestley on Air* .. gilt' while 'Zimmerman's *Zoology*' was bound in calf and gilt. These accounts also reveal that not all books bound are listed in the 1775 catalogue and the accounts for binding must be studied to obtain a more complete picture of purchases.

Natural History Books

Constable's enthusiasm for botany and natural history could seemingly be well satisfied by Benjamin White. For example the 1784 list includes No.48 of William Curtis *Flora Londinensis* (col'd) the first, but sadly not completed, British flora to be illustrated - with beautifully hand coloured life size engravings. Constable was a subscriber to this ambitious venture and in 1789 wrote his own alphabetical index to the 'five volumes of Curtis's Col'd plants', which has recently been discovered in his Hortus Siccus.[180] Linnaeus 'System of vegetables no.4' and Curtis 'catalogue' (to his botanic garden) also occur in White's list. They are typical purchases for a man ever eager to learn more about Linnaean principles and how they were adapted by followers such as Curtis. Earlier Constable had also purchased the works of other European botanists such as Boerhaave and Tournefort. The latters title of the 2 volume *History of plants growing about Paris* (translated into English by John Martyn London 1732) recalls Constable's botanising visit to Paris in 1742, the volume bearing Constable's bookplate is now in the Lindley library.

Indeed a considerable number of books have been long sold including some notable manuscripts acquired by William Constable, discussed elsewhere. However enough remains to make the realisation of Constable's epithet possible, found in notebook 'vol.1.' p.77: 'Inscrip. for a Library Trans: Each pleasing Art Lends Softness to the mind & with our studies are our Lives refind.'

CHAPTER TWELVE

A CENTURY OF CONSTABLE PATRONAGE - THE HULL FURNITURE INDUSTRY

Patronage

The patronage of successive generations of the Constable family was given with an even hand to those in their locality and to the London men. In part they consciously accepted an obligation to support the local economy, in part they knew that albeit with greater effort, they could achieve a fashionable effect at much less cost. On the other hand there was the undeniable glamour of famous London names.

The Constable's patronage of furniture makers is a well documented microcosm of the rise and maturing of a once important local industry, which steadily left its older centres such as York or Beverley to regroup in the increasingly prosperous Hull or Leeds. Families such as the Constables not only encouraged higher standards of manufacture, they introduced new or fashionable ideas at critical moments, often as in this case incidentally, helping the more ambitious to expand from the home into the export market through their Francophile tastes. Once such patronage is discontinued, and there is a lull in the export market, then, as in Hull post-1918, the industry will wither away.

In all, William Constable bought furniture from at least thirty makers in Beverley, York and Hull, but as the last grew in prosperity and developed in sophistication, more and more of his commissions went there. On the other hand, he also employed on a regular basis men such as Thomas Higham, or later Taylor and Bird, who supplied the architectural joinery, bookcases and so forth, made in the Burton Constable workshops, and one at least of the estate 'apprentices', John Lowry, went on to London as a journeyman, and set up business in the capital. In many cases, these local suppliers simply worked in wood as carpenters, joiners or furniture makers, that is they could not afford to turn away humbler tasks in the hope that more interesting work would come their way. They kept in touch with changing fashions by subscribing to or buying post publication some of the many pattern books available from the 1740's onward. Three at least subscribed to Thomas Chippendale's *'Director'*: George Reynoldson, his former apprentice Richard Farrer, and Edward Elwick, and all were significant suppliers to Constable. In a later generation, two of the Hull subscribers to Thomas Sheraton's Cabinet Dictionary supplied furniture to Burton Constable - Chapman & Son, and George Simpson. The cheaper pattern books did not rely upon subscribers for their publication costs, and their spread of ownership among craftsmen cannot now be determined, but Constable bought several, among them Ince & Mayhew's *'Universal System'*, and these he could show or lend to craftsmen as required. Robert and James Adams' *'Works in Architecture'*, whose earlier parts were collected by Constable (but left in their wrappers) - showed both interiors and their furniture at just the moment when Constable was commissioning designs for his Great Drawing Room, a task finally shared between James Wyatt and Thomas Chippendale, with most of the carved woodwork by Jeremiah Hargrave of Hull. The grossly overworked Wyatt had probably never met his patron - an early bill was addressed to 'Burton Constable Esqr' - nor visited the house. Had he done so, he would not have designed semi-circular or segmented table frames to support the rectangular tops Constable had just bought in Italy. At first, the error passed unnoticed, and Hargrave carved the mirror frames to fit the mirror plates supplied by Wyatt, but these were discarded (though paid for) before Chippendale was called in to redesign both the table frames and the mirrors. Wyatt's plates were retained, but with added head and side plates. Since the architect's drawings were not indicated at full size, this left Hargrave able to devise and carve the smaller scale details on his own.[181]

About sixty local makers are known to have supplied furniture and furnishings to Burton Constable between c.1740 and c.1870, a number about equally divided before and after 1800. In some cases, only one or two items were bought; in others, Hull firms such as Thomas Church, Jeremiah and Joseph Hargrave, or Thomas and Robert Walker, were active over a longer period with William Constable as their patron, while in the 1830's and 1840's, it was Thomas Ward (pl.4), and his apprentice, Thomas Wilkinson Wallis, who were most active, chiefly for Lady Marianne Clifford Constable, while for her successor Lady Rosina, it was the Richardsons who gained most of her commissions. This steady and continuous patronage over so long a period brought with it several advantages for the locality. The work was carried out with good materials and to a high standard of craftsmanship, thus encouraging the supply of both within the area, while at the same time, the craftsman was offered the opportunity to expand his skills as a designer as well as a manufacturer, or if the design was given by others, then the latter was at least fashionable and sometimes avant garde by the London standards of the day. Such patronage, skilfully deployed by the craftsman, could be used by them to advertise themselves to other potential clients in the vicinity, usually by encouraging visitors to see work in progress. At the same time, the earlier local centres of production, e.g. Beverley or York, declined, as Hull or Leeds attracted their more ambitious men, e.g. Jeremiah Hargrave or Thomas Walker, to these rapidly growing towns with their increasingly prosperous inhabitants. Some craftsmen, e.g. John Lowry, went as journeymen to London, and did not return; others, such as Thomas Brooks, made the round journey. Others again, like Thomas Wilkinson Wallis, struggled hard to win international notice at the Great Exhibition of 1851, but were not able to exploit that special opportunity to the full and remained close to their birth place, having briefly and unhappily sampled the wider world.

That William Constable had confidence in his suppliers there is little question, but he must have been made aware of the limitations of the smaller firms, so that rather than wait substantial periods for the completion of his orders, he selected a series of firms to work for him concurrently. Something of the time taken, and the methods used to produce specific items of furniture can be seen from the maker's bills. Thus Joseph Foster sometimes, states the number of days needed to produce each item and[182] that he bought his mahogany plank ready cut from William Luccock of Hull, who also supplied Foster with 'mahogany feneer'. Foster also lists all his other costs for materials and tools. Jeremiah Hargrave, perhaps making out a bill for the steward on the spot, itemises his own employees names, the time each had spent to the nearest hour, and 'the profits etc'. This type of information, though no doubt repeated elsewhere, is made more interesting because the relevant items remain at Burton Constable.

The detailed organisation of the various types of furniture suppliers seem to have had little study and this is especially true of the usually smaller provincial firms though the field is a steadily gaining recognition and the results of recent research are reaching publication. The Gillow archives do of course reveal in the greatest detail the operation of one of England's largest furniture makers, but firms who employed a wide range of craftsmen could and did encourage piecework to increase their output. The Hull firms, by contrast, were small and their owners had to rely upon others for a wide range of tasks outside their own narrow speciality. This dependence was clearly a disadvantage to an ambitious man. From the Burton Constable archives, however, it is possible to trace the birth and flourishing of what became one of Hull's major industries. Thus in 1737, mahogany had to be specially ordered and brought up from London. By the 1760's, there were public auctions of mahogany logs on the quayside, and within a decade there were importers such as Dixon and Moxon specialising in exotic hardwoods, a trade that indicated, not merely the rapid rise in the prosperity of Hull as a town, but also makes clear that the newly fledged furniture industry was expected to last. By 1794 it had in fact gained in reputation, for a Mr. Crust of Chancery Lane in London, was advertising jobs for such Hull journeymen in the *Hull Packet*.

26. *Side table by Jeremiah Hargrave after a design by Lightoler.*

27. *Dining chair by John Lowry of Hull and London.*

For the whole of the eighteenth century, every item of furniture was produced to order - whether for display in the shop of its maker, or for the individual client. Sometimes the latter obtained drawings from outside, for example from an architect, and these would become the basis upon which the craftsman would work. At Burton Constable, these drawings were chiefly the responsibility of the carver-architect Timothy Lightoler, but upon these, his patron, William Constable, grafted his own typically neo-classical ideas. This fusion of ideas from both architect and patron, the craftsman such as Jeremiah Hargrave had to put into execution, though it was to fail when Wyatt was the chosen architect, and here Thomas Chippendale succeeded Wyatt and Hargrave as both designer and executant. If necessary a model would be called for to clarify any doubts raised by sketches or drawings.

A century later, in the early 1870's, William Richardson sketched existing furniture at Burton Constable, including that by Chippendale, and devised new pieces that harmonised with Chippendale work, and with the pattern pieces 'got from Paris', in an expensive attempt to unify old and new.

Most of the eighteenth century firms were small family concerns that rarely lasted more than three generations. It was typical for many to begin as skilled tradesmen who found they had additional talents such as draughtsmanship and the ability to design. Thus carpenters/joiners/masons could and did become carvers/sculptors/architects. In Hull one may instance the Hargraves[183] or the Earles, or, within one person, Wallis, whose father was a grocer cum cabinet maker. The younger Wallis found it necessary to do the humblest ship carving, the higher grade of furniture or architectural carving, and the sculpture of the true 'artist'. Such compounding of skills was not always happy. Thomas Ward, who did much for Burton Constable, and was Wallis' master, was also the landlord of the 'Grapes', and with too easy an access to alcohol, became its victim. Wallis himself, though equal to his London rivals, lacked the confidence to fight back on their terms and finished his career, in Louth, as a sanitary inspector.

Other craftsmen saw Hull as a goal. James Piotti, an immigrant from Italy, settled first in Lincoln before being drawn to the greater prosperity of Hull. Other Italians who settled in Hull, such as Maspoli or Taroni, also worked for Sir Clifford Constable.

This influx of furniture makers had a noticeable impact upon the timber trade of Hull which, though of longstanding importance, was primarily concerned with timber of north European origin. By the 1730's, however, particular orders for exotic timbers such as mahogany could be arranged via London timber importers who sent the small quantities involved via the coastal trade. In 1737, for example 5 planks of mahogany were bought when Cuthbert Constable was creating the first section of the New Gallery, and more mahogany continued to be bought as his son chose that wood instead of painted softwood, for new doors, staircase handrailing, and so forth. In this change, the Constable's were not alone, as Hull's leading merchants also chose mahogany for their finer architectural joinery, culminating with major new developments such as those in Charlotte Stréet (now George Street) of the 1780's, where the finest mahogany was typically selected for the doors of all the principal reception rooms, and some of the more generous staircases such as that of the Pease House. In the 1760's however, the Hull mahogany trade was intermittent, but as the furniture trade rapidly developed, this uncertainty in the flow of a basic raw material proved unsatisfactory, and new specialist merchants arose, such as Dixon and Moxon's, who, via the network of waterways dependent upon the Humber, also transhipped mahogany throughout the port's extensive hinterland, which included not only much of Yorkshire, but Lincolnshire, Nottinghamshire, and parts of Derbyshire as well. The establishment of these new timber yards tempted the more enterprising furniture makers to set up business in the new built streets such as Savile Street or Bond Street which were close to the west end of Queen's Dock.

This concentration of business meant that the extra cost of transport to Beverley and York put their furniture makers at an expensive disadvantage against which they had no compensating advantage. Equally the more enterprising Hull makers had the further benefit of easy access to the export trade, one which they were skilfully to deploy as Free Trade advanced in scope during the nineteenth century. These new markets, especially those of France and Germany, meant that the Hull makers worked in the French as well as the English manner, a style early introduced into Hull through the Constable's.

The growth of national prosperity had, however, begun to outstrip the resources of craftsmen from the 1760's, with the result that many turned to alternative materials that were cheaply and easily manufactured, especially for the furniture trade. They included the synthetic material called 'composition'. This was at first imported into Hull from York, where it was manufactured by firms such as the Blakesleys or the Wolstenholmes. William Settle of Savile Street advertised in the *Hull Packet* of 2nd(?) July 1795 that he distributed the Wolstenholme product which he claimed was 'better by 70 per cent than those manufactured in Hull'. Twenty years earlier, the Chippendales had used a few 'composition' ornaments on their furniture (of 1777-1778) for the Great Drawing Room of Burton Constable, but it was not until the era of Sir Clifford Constable that composition ornament began to dominate parts of the furniture trade. Wallis, in his autobiography, tells us how he mastered the art of cutting the necessary moulds, envisaging the outcome whilst actually cutting out the reverse image.[184] Both Wallis' master, Thomas Ward, and his close rival, Thomas Brooks, used 'composition' extensively, thus substantially reducing the cost of very richly ornamented items such as the palm tree cornerstands on the staircase landings. These were then gilded, and any difference between real carved work and its moulded substitute was visually concealed. Some bills of the day specify 'composition'; many, with less honesty, preferred still to call it 'carved' work. Well within Wallis' lifetime, the vogue for 'composition' declined, and there was a return either to the traditional gesso on wood, for gilded pieces, or a variety of exotic woods, inlaid or polished to reveal their own beauties. Such pieces predominate among the huge quantities of furniture provided by the Richardsons. In their heyday - the 1860's

and 70's - woods from both the East and West Indies were fashionable, as steam-powered ships drastically cut the journey time from the Far East. This worldwide supply of raw materials was paralleled by a similar approach to design. For example, Owen Jones' *'Grammar of Ornament'* (1856) was truly international in its choice of models, one of which, plate 42 . . . . was of a Moorish pattern from the Court of the Fish Pond at the Alhambra in Spain. This was paraphrased to serve as the design for the cover of the 'Alhambra' chair bought for £10 from the Richardsons in 1870. Richardson pretentiously described the painted and gilded decoration as 'illuminated'. As a successful manufacturer for both home and export markets, he sought to bring attention to that success by occupying one of the showier new villas facing on the Pearson Park, its facade enriched with much carving. In later years if may be noted this was occupied by one of the Ranks who, in their earliest days had supplied the Constable's with flour from their windmill in Holderness Road. The Ranks were followed by the French Convent and its School, prior to its recent demolition.

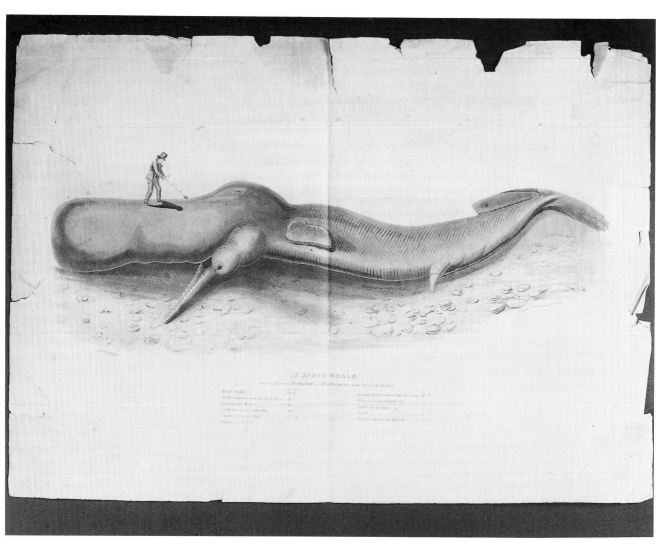

28. *The sperm whale stranded at Tunstall in 1825, the skeleton of which was erected in the grounds of Burton Constable.*

CHAPTER THIRTEEN

THE BURTON CONSTABLE WHALE

As Lord Paramount of the Seigniory of Holderness the Squire of Burton Constable Hall had rights to the carcase of any whale stranded on the coast of his territory, both along the eastern seaboard and within the Humber.[185] Stranded whales and sturgeon were normally considered 'royal fish' but the prerogative of the crown was sometimes relinquished in favour of a local potentate. The Prince Bishops of the county palatine of Durham had similar rights and the skeletal remains of a fifty foot sperm whale washed ashore at Seaton Carew in 1766 can still be seen in the undercroft of Durham Cathedral.[186] Only one of the scores of cetaceans which must have been stranded on the East Yorkshire coast over the centuries has achieved any kind of celebrity.[187] This also was a sperm whale which came ashore at Tunstall in the Spring of 1825. The first report appears in the *Hull Advertiser* for 6 May after it had been observed by several local fishermen afloat in the sea. Assuming it to be still alive they kept clear to avoid any possibility of damage being inflicted on their small craft. Eventually the dead animal beached beneath the low mud cliffs some threequarters of a mile north of Tunstall. Cetaceans of a wide variety of species, including pilot whales, bottle nose dolphins and rorquals, still come ashore in this area but animals of the magnitude of this bull sperm whale are rare. The whale attracted a good deal of attention and on the Sunday after the stranding nearly a thousand people came to see it. Unfortunately the several days delay before news of the creature reached Hull allowed putrefaction to advance and no doubt the carcase was considerably mutilated by the hoards of sightseers. A partial dissection was however undertaken by Dr. James Alderson[188] and the newspaper gives an account of the result; telling us that the eyes were remarkably small, the surface being not much more than those of a bullock and 'the shape of the eye (which we had the opportunity of seeing removed from the head), is peculiar, being nearly

in the form of a truncated cone. When one of the cavities of the head was cut open it yielded about 18 gallons of spermaceti, it was perfectly fluid and limpid, having much the appearance of clear olive oil but immediately on its being exposed to the air, it began to congeal, and in a short time became opake (*Sic*) and solid'.

Another account from the *Hull Rockingham*, the following day, 7 May, records the length of the animal as 58ft 6in (17.8m) from the nose to 'the end of the division of the tail'. There were forty-seven teeth in the lower jaw, corresponding with sockets in the upper jaw, 24 on the left, 23 on the right. The span of the tail flukes was 14ft (4.2m) and a rudimentary dorsal fin rose up about a foot and terminated in a hook-like process posteriorly. Its blowhole, situated near the extremity of the head was slightly to the left of the median line. On a more commerical note the body was said to be covered in a layer of blubber 10/12in (0.25 to 0.3m) thick worth about £500 when flensed and boiled to extract the oil. No wound or pathological condition that could be held responsible for the whales death was discovered, in the course of dissection only 'one spear of a sword fish, penetrating several inches . . . but this could hardly affect vitality'. A 'bucketful' of cuttle bones was retrieved from the stomach (*Hull Rockingham*, 14 May, 1825).

Dr. Alderson read a paper to the Cambridge Philosophical Society on the 16 May 1825, barely more than a week after his dissection and 'An account of a whale of the Spermaceti tribe cast on the Yorkshire coast' was published some two years later. There are several representations of the whale all of which apparently derive from sketches made on the beach by Richard Iveson, steward to the Constable family. The best illustration is an aquatint engraved by Fenner of London and the printed legend tells us when the beast first arrived on the beach, 'Cast on shore at Turnstall (*sic*) in Holderness on 28 April 1825.[189] The inscription is followed by details of the dimensions and it is interesting to note that the artist depicts a gentleman standing on the top of the animal holding a surveyors measuring wheel or 'way-wiser'. Essentially the same picture is seen in a contemporary lithograph which is clearly a more cheaply produced print intended for sale to a wider public.[190] It bears the legend 'Spermaceti whale, length 58ft 6 inches. Cast on the Holderness coast 28 April 1825'. The eye is moved, incorrectly nearer to the top of the head giving the creature a silly smiling expression. Both pictures show the sad state of one of the great whales after it has left its natural element, the rib cage collapsed, the body flaccid and lacking the natural tension of a living animal. Dr. Alderson's scientific paper uses essentially the same illustration but accompanied by a full length dorsal view of the whale and drawings of the skull, jaws, eye and one of the cuttlefish bones found in the stomach.[191] All of these were lithographed after sketches by Christopher Alderson, elder brother of James. Dissection also revealed a further two teeth which had not broken through the surface of the gum but were buried in the right side of the jaw, making a total of 49.

An offprint of Dr. Aldersons paper bound in red leather and titled in gold letters, 'An account of the S. Whale cast on shore at Tunstall, 1825' is preserved in the library of Burton Constable Hall. It is inscribed on one of the blank sheets at the beginning:-

'To Sir Thomas Ashton Clifford Constable Baronet this short notice of the spermaceti whale, the skeleton of which has been articulated by his direction and which forms a valuable specimen of natural history unique in Great Britain, is presented by his obliged and obedient humble servant James Alderson'.[192]

Strandings of all kinds of cetaceans have occurred throughout history often as a result of being caught by severe weather in shallow coastal waters. Most landed in remote and sparsely populated regions and while the local inhabitants may have marvelled at their size and strangeness they were rather more interested in these creatures as an unexpected windfall of meat and oil. Even the bones would find practical use, a vertebra might be turned into a chopping block or stool and the jaw bones and ribs into building materials. Down to modern times Eskimo have used whale bones in the construction of the roofs of their semi-subterranean houses of stones and turves.

In the Middle Ages when a stranding occurred near a major centre of population it would attract great interest from all sections of society. A particularly fine engraving by Jan Sanreadam of a sperm whale on the shore at Beverwijk on the Dutch coast in 1601 shows Count Ernst Casimir of Nassau and his entourage in the foreground and a great gathering of people round about.[193] Writing in his diary for 3 June 1658 John Evelyn tells us of a whale caught in the shallows of the Thames near Greenwich 'which drew an infinite concourse to see it, by water, horse, coach and on foot, from London and all parts.[194] The description makes it clear that it was a large specimen of a North Atlantic or Biscay Right Whale.

Beached cetaceans still continue to make news, mass strandings of pilot whales are usually widely reported in the media. In recent times complete whale carcases preserved with formalin have been taken on tour throughout Europe, the 'Gigantic Whale Exhibition' in 1901 and 'Jonas the Whale' in 1952 are two instances. These were both examples of the Blue Whale, not only the biggest of the whales but the largest animal ever to have lived on earth.

Despite the interest aroused by the whale tribe our knowledge of them remained sketchy until this century. Aristotle writing in the fourth century before Christ gives us the first detailed description of any cetacean, namely the dolphin, and he was a discerning enough observer to realise it was not a fish but an air-breathing mammal. The compilation of nature lore by Pliny the Elder, who met his end during the eruption of Vesuvius in AD79, however, bequeathed to the Middle Ages an altogether confusing picture of whales and their habits.

Perhaps the cetacean most familiar to western Europe was the common porpoise which was extensively traded as a source of food. It was this animal which became the subject of the first recorded whale dissection undertaken in 1654 by Bartholinus, professor of anatomy at Copenhagen. The English naturalist John Ray dissected a porpoise brain in 1671 but it was the eminent surgeon John Hunter (1728-93) who made the first major survey of cetacean anatomy. Working on whole carcases of some of the smaller whales and portions of the tissues and organs of some of the great whales provided by his medical and scientific confreres he published the results in the transactions of the Royal Society in 1787.[195]

Another surgeon, Thomas Beale (1807-49) became interested in the sperm whale after a spell as ships doctor in a South Sea whaler.[196] He published his initial account in a slim pamphlet entitled 'A Few Observations on the Natural History of the Sperm Whale' which was issued in 1835. As a result of this his attention was brought to the skeleton of the Tunstall whale, still preserved at Burton Constable Hall, by Mr. Pearsall, the then curator of the museum of the Hull Literary and Philosophical Society. It had apparently only just recently been articulated and set up in the grounds of the house by Edward Wallis, surgeon and lecturer in anatomy and physiology at the Hull School of Medicine.[197] Beale arranged with Sir Clifford Constable[198] to examine the bones and he consulted with Wallis on the structure of the whale trachea. He also saw on the Lit. and Phil. Society's premises the skeletons of a bottlenose whale, a porpoise and the blue whale which had been washed ashore in the Humber in 1835. As a result of his observations, illuminating discussions with the local cognoscenti, as well as reference to Dr. Aldersons published paper Beale was able to publish a much fuller account in the book which was published in 1839. Entitled *The Natural History of the Sperm Whale* it also incorporated an account of his South Sea whaling experiences, 1830-3.

This volume was widely read both for its scientific information and the details of the prosecution of the South Sea fishery. It became a major source for *Moby Dick*, Herman Melville's celebrated story of Capt. Ahab's obsessive pursuit of the great white whale. The copy which Melville owned and annotated is still extant and the descriptions of the habits of the whale, its anatomy and methods of hunting it were utilised to great effect by the American writer in his literary masterpiece. This celebrated book is really two in one, the principal theme of Ahab's search for the mighty sperm whale which had snapped off his leg, interspersed with chapters concerning the history of whaling and the characteristics of the cetacean family. The basic factual information is invariably developed and distorted as Melville teases and pokes fun at the learned authors of his sources and elaborates his raw material into someting satirical or fantastical.

In the chapter entitled 'A Bower in the Arsacides' is a passage which not only immortalises the Burton Constable whale but also the museum of the Hull Literary and Philosophical Society:[199]

'There is a Leviathanic Museum they tell me, in Hull, England, one of the whaling ports of that country, where they have some fine specimens of fin-backs and other whales ... Moreover at a place in Yorkshire, England, Burton Constable by name, a certain Sir Clifford Constable has in his possession the skeleton of a Sperm Whale but of moderate size, by no means of the full grown magnitude of my friend King Tranquos. In both cases, the stranded whales were originally claimed by their proprietors upon similar grounds. King Tranquo seizing his because he wanted it: and Sir Clifford, because he was lord of the seignories of those parts. Sir Clifford's whale had been articulated throughout; so that, like a great chest of drawers you can open and shut him, in all his bony cavities - spread out his ribs like a gigantic fan - and swing all day upon his lower jaw. Locks are to be put upon some of his trapdoors and shutters; and a footman will show round future visitors with a bunch of keys at his side. Sir Clifford thinks of charging two pence for a peep at the whispering galley in the spinal column; three pence to hear the echo at the hollow of his cerebellum and six pence for the unrivalled view from his forehead'.[200]

King Tranquo is an invention of course, a native prince of an exotic Pacific Island whose proprietorial rights over stranded whales is counterpointed to those of a Yorkshire gentleman. The mechanical contrivances of the Burton Constable skeleton are fantasy, a charming literary conceit, and as far as can be ascertained it was simply articulated with a rod through the vertebrae and the skull and spine resting on a series of stanchions set in the ground. The specimen was erected a little to the south of the house in what is called the 'Whale Belt' but sadly the assemblage has fallen into ruin and now only a scatter of rotten bones obscured by grass and weeds can be discerned poking through the surface of the soil.[201] Surprisingly perhaps there is no known illustration of the whale *in situ* and it seems to have gone unnoticed and unrecorded by nineteenth travellers. Burton Constable is somewhat remote, some seven miles to the east of Hull near Sproatley but it does seem strange that it was so quickly forgotten and allowed to decay. A large tooth of this sperm whale was donated to the Hull museums by Major R. Chichester-Constable and can now be seen displayed in the Town Docks Museum while a large number of whale teeth preserved at Burton Constable presumably belonged to the same animal. An undated newspaper cutting, probably c.1870, in the Burton Constable archive kept in the County Record Office at Beverley, includes a short account of the whale with a paragraph as follows 'In the porch at Burton Constable, near Hull, is the skeleton of a whale which was cast ashore on the Holderness coast about half a century ago'. Presumably the skeleton had already collapsed and some portions of it had been brought into the house.

Surgeon Wallis' other great specimen, the blue whale, was transferred from the Literary and Philosophical Society's museum in the Assembly Rooms[202] to the Royal Institution which was inaugurated by Prince Albert in 1854. Washed up near the entrance to the Humber in 1835 it measured 47ft. 6in (14.5m) in length and the head contained 580 plates of whalebone (baleen). Published by Dr. J.E.Gray in 1847 it was the first of the species to be scientifically described and therefore became the type specimen of all Blue Whales.[203] At the opening of the new fisheries museum in 1912 most of the cetacean material was transferred from the Albion Street establishment, except the Blue Whale which remained in the Royal Institution until 1935. Since 1901 the museum of the Literary and Philosophical Society has been in the care of the Hull Corporation [204] and it was decided that this important specimen should become part of the na-

tional collections at the Natural History museum in South Kensington.[205]

Edward Wallis remained in Hull for the remainder of his life and we can learn nothing further of his career. Dr. James Alderson however, left his native city to achieve considerable distinction in the medical profession.

Along with Wallis, R. Craven and R. Harvey he was responsible for the establishing of the Hull School of Anatomy and Medicine in 1831 became senior physician to St. Mary's Hospital, Paddington in 1851 and consulting physician to the same institution soon after being elected president of the Royal College of Physicians in 1867. Knighted in 1869 he was appointed physician extraordinary to Queen Victoria in 1874 and was elected a Fellow of the Royal Society. Among his publications was a work on diseases of the stomach and alimentary canal' (1847) and papers contributed to the transactions of the Royal Society and the Medico-Chirugical Society. A marble bust of Sir James displayed in the entrance to the old Hull Royal Infirmary until its demolition in 1972 now sits on its pedestal in the whaling gallery of the Town Docks Museum. His former home, erected in Albion Street c.1846, which became the Church Institute and then suffered many years of neglect has recently (Summer 1991) been refurbished and opened as a public house called 'The Institute'.

CHAPTER FOURTEEN

SIR CLIFFORD CONSTABLE, HIS FIRST WIFE LADY MARIANNE, AND THEIR FURNITURE

Two types of furniture makers can be identified from the accounts at Burton Constable - the craftsman who does everything within his workshop and the carver-maker who prefers to get another to do the joinery before adding the detail himself. This latter interdependence is explicit for men such as Jeremiah Hargrave (d.1784) though his bills never identify his chosen joiner by name. Hargrave must have provided the joiner with drawings sufficiently detailed to allow the latter to make the item even when for example the architect Lightoler, had initiated the idea. Sixty years later a combination of sources can be traced. Firstly the Constables studied Brighton Pavilion, possibly buying one of the books illustrating that royal extravaganza, and such would be shown to Hull makers such as Thomas Ward (pl.4). An idea would then be amplified with a sketch by Lady Marianne and this would be worked up by Ward, who then got Carlill to prepare the 'blank'. Ward then asked his apprentice Thomas Wilkinson Wallis (1821-1903) to do the necessary carving at a cost of £31.10.0. as in the case of the dragon chair, or share the work, as in the '2 Cheval Screen frames Cut for Carvin' (Sent to Mr. Ward £1.14.0 Sept. 1840). This 'carvin' was in fact modelled 'composition', a material much cheaper than genuinely hand carved wood. The two screens are still together and as Wallis noted, his master admitted that his apprentice's work was superior, and on another occasion that without Wallis, Ward could not carry on his business.[206]

Thomas Wallis was therefore offered a weekly wage of 24 shillings, 4 shillings less than his brother was earning in a similar capacity at Constantines in Leeds. Having worked for a short time for that firm, he concluded he preferred to work for less money in his home town. When Wards were busy, Wallis would work from 5am to 10pm with overtime paid at 3d-4d per hour. The normal day was 6am to 7pm. As an apprentice, Wallis recorded that 'I carefully regulated my food. Two small pieces of bread with a cup full of milk served for my breakfast. The same quantity of bread with two cupfuls of weak tea for my five o'clock meal a very small quantity of meat at dinner and no alcoholic drink'. A good workman then earned 4/6 per day.

Unlike more prosperous tradesmen who charged the Constables for horse-hire, in William Constable's day it was 2/6d or 3/, Wallis walked the nine miles to and from Burton Constable, where he saw the latest purchases from Paris, some of them secondhand, including a gilded table and two chairs. These Wallis had to clean down, regesso and regild, using the 'drawing room' as a workshop. In between such commissions Wallis had to work as a ship's carver, then still an important source of potential income. At Gibson's shipyard he was 'designing the pattern as I went on'. Wallis sketched from nature, and, at home, set up a small bench to improve his carving. He started at 4am 'before going to my days work at the shop' - where work started at 6am.

'About this time Lady Constable made a rough design to a small scale for a chair; it was composed of six dragons - part of their crest. They were twisted about so as to form four legs the two arms and the back - Mr. Ward was proud that the work had been done by his late apprentice, he showed it to many people, amongst others to Mr. Chalmers, then Mayor of Hull who admired it very much, and anticipated that the young carver would rise in his profession. I thought & more praise was given to the young carver than he deserved'.[207] In 1841-2, facing unemployment, Wallis went to London to buy the best carving tools and incidentally to see the carved work of Grinling Gibbons. In 1850 he exhibited at the Society of Arts, where he gained the Silver Medal, the Great Exhibition of 1851, the Paris Exhibition of 1855, and the 1862 International Exhibition in London and in both cities he gained further medals. The *Illustrated Catalogue* of the 1862 exhibition names 'our best connoisseurs who gave Wallis encouragement': Mr. Tomline of Orwell Park, Messrs. S. Ashton, J.W. Turner & J. Carlton, all of Manchester, R. Napier of Shandon, Lord Beecher, Lord Carrington, Russell-Gurney and A. Varden and others.[208](pl.7)

Meanwhile, Wallis's brother, Samuel reported that in the west of Yorkshire the people were starving and that many who were desperate deliberately stole food rather than perish. Wallis's master died a drunkard in 1850 and soon after the Constable's began to patronise the Richardsons.

Lady Marianne also bought 'Old English' furniture: for example, a part set of carved walnut high-backed chairs, had them gilded, and further matching chairs made and gilded to match. Here her aim was to help create an 'Old English' atmosphere in the Long Gallery. The new chairs could be made of pine not walnut, because the gilding would wholly conceal the inferior wood.

In William Constable's day interesting furniture would be bought at auction sales rather than in 'antique' shops, but in Lady Marianne's time such shops were both well established and fashionable, whether in London or Paris. Thus in 1781 he asked the Hull cabinet-maker Thomas Walker to attend the auction sale at Lairgate Hall, Beverley, to bid for its most expensive furniture. Walker succeeded in buying Sir James Pennyman's best bed for £90.15.0. No comparable purchase at auction has been traced for the nineteenth century.

In September 1833 Wallis' master, Thomas Ward, was gessoing and gilding the japanned chairs Chippendale had supplied in 1774, and regilding and extending the tripod stands attributable to the Chippendale commission of 1778. The latter furnitire was also the model chosen by the later Hull furniture makers Messrs. Richardson, who, for Lady Rosina, extended the suite that was to be sent to Dunbar House in 1869-70.

Lady Rosina

By chance the vouchers as well as the account books survive, the former revealing so much more information, but the purchases of Lady Rosina culminated in a case in the Court of Chancery. The firm of Richardson and Sons then at 33-35 Bond Street, Hull, were founded in 1812, during the Napoleonic War, and were finally bombed out in an air raid upon Hull in 1915. According to J.J. Sheahan, the Richardsons were by 1866 'the largest Furniture Manufactory in the kingdom - Every article of first class furniture suitable either for the church, the palace or the mansion is designed and manufactured here upon the rough log, and carved out to the utmost finish and polish!' The Constable's patronage culminated in the huge commission of 1869-71, offered to them by Lady Rosina Clifford Constable, Sir Clifford's second wife. By then, the fashionable styles had become even more eclectic. In place of late Georgian revivals of the 'Elizabethan' Louis XIV, and Louis XV and the late incursion into the Chinese style, there was the revival of the Louis XVI, the Empire and as an exotic contrast, the Moorish. Unusually this was compounded at Burton Constable by the specific attempt to harmonise some of this new furniture with that made for the house by the Chippendales. Unfortunately for the Constables, Lady Rosina corrupted most of her suppliers, and the papers of the resulting court case reveal, for the historian, just how far a prosperous firm was prepared to go in order to secure business.

The most obvious change between the Burton Constable furniture of the 1830's and 1860's was the revival in the use of fine woods. Excluding the gilded furniture, most of Lady Marianne's purchases had been of painted furniture either unmistakably as for example beds painted drab and blue, or items painted or stained to look like oak or rosewood. In the second phase, oak, ebony, walnut, thuya and mahogany pieces were inlaid with contrasting woods such as holly or purple wood and then mounted with ormolu. To show off these exotic timbers to better advantage, the lines of the pieces were simplified. The carved scroll work and the asymmetrical line gave place to the turned leg and geometrical frame. It was opulence of another kind, for with its small scale ornament and variety of rich materials, it was as obviously showy. No less interesting - where the best 18th century carvers such as Jeremiah Hargrave could equal their

London rivals, so too a century later could the Richardsons.(pls.9-12)

It unfortunately remains true that however highly skilled, those craftsmen who choose to remain working in provincial centres, such as Hull, will be undervalued in comparison to their metropolitan counterparts.[209] It is equally true that even higher standards were achieved by the French. One instance can be noted here: The Duval pattern chair 'got from Paris' was copied by the Richardsons, but it should be observed how much more delicate and meaningful is the carved cresting of the French chair than that of its English counterpart. The former has a bow and arrow and floral emblems of chaste love, while the English one, two sprays of coarser roses and a cartouche. In all other respects one could not distinguish between the original and the copy, for the French liking for walnut, and the typical English use of mahogany, cannot be seen when as here both are fully gilded.

Through their exporting contacts, the Richardsons were well able to satisfy the Constable's Francophile tastes on the one hand, while ingenious enough to design pieces that specifically harmonised with those already at Burton Constable on the other. This linkage was important then because furniture from Burton Constable was refurbished and taken down to Dunbar House, Teddington while, thirty or so years later, the new Teddington furniture was brought to Burton Constable after having been taken to Italy in the interim. The self-conscious harmonization between old and new may, however, have been a convenient and flattering ploy in an attempt to cajole Sir Clifford into assent, that is, it was 'theirs' rather than simply 'hers'.

29. *Copy of Duval chair by Richardson of Hull.*

CHAPTER FIFTEEN

SIR CLIFFORD AND HIS SECOND WIFE LADY ROSINA - AN OVERLAP OF TASTE

The Court Case of 1871

The extraordinary story of Sir Clifford's final years has emerged through the Court case of 1871. Lady Rosina Constable - alias Mrs. Montague or Rosina Brandon, had become Sir Clifford's mistress before Lady Marianne's death in 1862, but the couple married in 1865 and thereafter Rosina seems to have schemed how best to secure her eventual widowhood without regard to the then parlous finances of Sir Clifford's estate. The latter's will was to stipulate that Lady Rosina would be entitled to take anything she wanted out of Burton Constable for her own use during her lifetime, but following her death, those items would have to be returned to Sir Clifford's heirs.

Rosina persuaded her husband to spend £6,500 on a Thames side villa in Broom Road at Teddington as a love nest. No expense was to be spared in re-equipping 'Dunbar House' as it was renamed, indoors or out, the final total spent amounting to £37,000. The gardens were designed by Goldrings and furnished with every kind of plant by Messrs. Veitch of Chelsea, and where the public road crossed the garden between the villa and the Thames, Lady Rosina ordered it to be relaid with the same blue gravel as that of the garden paths, despite the objection of the local highway surveyor.

The furnishings of Dunbar House was extravagant, even by high Victorian standards of opulent luxury, and much of that furnishing found its way to Burton Constable only after 1900. Sir Clifford's patronage was thus tripartite, the restoration of the house and its furniture in the 1830's and early 1840's, a process of new and 'antique' French, Italian and German furnishings during their Continental journeys of the same period, much of this now not capable of positive documentation; and the second bout of refurbishment under the sway of Lady Rosina. Sometimes she ordered the embellishment of existing items bought earlier by Lady Marianne, more often she also commissioned new pieces, almost all from Hull.

The furniture brought to Burton Constable by William Constable and the successive wives of Sir Clifford have this much in common - their Francophile taste, and the willingness to order important pieces from Hull makers as well as those in London. They differ in that where William brought 'Antiques' believing them to be of Roman date, for Lady Marianne the word meant pieces from no further back than the late seventeenth century. For her, as for many contemporaries, it was enough that her purchases had once been at Versailles or some other elegant French chateau despoiled during the French Revolution.

This interlocking of different national styles, periods and pieces is a characteristic of Burton Constable, and owes its mainspring to two influences not usually found together in an English house. Firstly, because the Constables had remained with the Old Faith, they had been forced to seek their education abroad, usually in France, and thus in their formative years, they had imbibed a taste for French culture that was quite independent of the more familiar Grand Tour. They went on these journeys as well. Secondly, they, like many other contemporary patrons, felt some obligation to help and encourage the leading local craftsmen, not as was so often the case, by granting them the order for the lesser items, but rather in giving them the chance to execute the major items as well. Given a willing patron on the one hand and an ambitious craftsman on the other, both could achieve satisfaction. The Constables were to prove lucky in that their chosen craftsmen could rise to the opportunities offered, and to perform with a technical skill at least equal to that of their London counterparts. in William Constable's day, they were promptly paid, and they prospered accordingly.

In the nineteenth century, while the local patronage

was generous enough, the matter of payment became ever more fraught. One may be tempted into excusing overcharging by acknowledging that, for example, Lady Rosina wanted work executed quickly but to special order, whilst it was known that the Constables of that generation were bad payers, and these factors, taken together, suggested that a partial payment of an overcharge would being in more cash than a similar percentage of a reasonable demand. If the evidence of the Chancery case was indeed true, either the widely differing, geographicaly dispersed suppliers were in collusion, or they severally concluded that a partial payment of an overcharge was at least some answer to an undoubted problem. It seems typical of overcharging that every item is fulsomely and lengthily described as if to justify the sums demanded.

Ironically, the very length and detail of the descriptions did, however, prove to be ready ammunition for those conducting the cross examination during the Chancery hearing. Thus an item described as 'got from Paris' could as well be a cheaper English copy of a sample sent from Paris. The influence of that capital city was indeed all pervading, albeit of the demi-monde of the Second Empire. Interestingly, Lady Rosina evidently disliked gaslight; her new Louis Seize revival chandeliers were just that, though with far more candle branches than usual for their eighteenth century counterparts. She cannot have seen anything ironic in her choice of Madonna lilies, the symbols par excellence of chastity, as the chief motif for a chandelier of one devoted to a life of unscrupulous sensuality, typified by her selection of a mirrored bed, case furniture, and doors. The last were totally covered by plate glass mirrors, cushioned with soft pads of india rubber and fitted with cut glass door furniture inset into silvered fittings.

Equally hypocritical, she ordered the legs of her chairs, sofas and chaise longues to be masked by fringing or drapery in compliance with the idea that the sight of an exposed leg was somehow immoral.

The parlous finances of the estate must have been known to her, but that was to be no deterrent to her vast expenditure. She was later to justify some of it by commenting that when visiting the showrooms of Messrs. Richardson with her then ailing husband, it was enough if he smiled at an item for that 'order' to be confirmed. The Richardsons quickly took advantage of the situation by discreetly announcing the various Constable commissions, and thus encouraging visitors to see work then in hand.

How different Lady Rosina from her predecessor Lady Marianne. The latter had when in Paris been introduced to a 'Duchesse' who responded with a polite charm. Lady Marianne was delighted and enquired from her family as to what present would best be suitable in return for such friendship. Her son and husband were alarmed that Marianne was so unworldly as not to know that this particular 'Duchesse' was merely the latest mistress of the Duke and that it was imperative for them to rescue Marianne from certain embarassment. Marianne had thought that a jet paper knife, bought in Scarborough, would be appropriate. The outcome is unrecorded.

Marianne, unlike her successor, genuinely charmed those who worked for her. She, like many of her generation, attempted to design as well as to draw. Poulson recorded in 1841 that Lady Constable had designed an Axminster carpet for her Boudoir,[210] and Wallis noted that the Chinese dragon chair was based upon one of her suggestions. Similarly, Lady Rosina, having ordered a piano from Erards for an estimated cost of £255 then kept raising the specification for the ornament of its case until the final cost was £787.10.0., including the cost of Buhlwork panels modelled upon the doors of a cabinet that had been imported by Lady Marianne.

On the South front Poulson described how Lady Marianne Constable furnished her boudoir to which was added a small conservatory, probably to the designs of Henry Lockwood, then of Hull. The Boudoir was a tent room, the walls and ceiling 'fluted with pink and white muslin, finished off with pink silk drapery, with the elegant and delicate monthly rose'. The roses were of porcelain. The obvious charm of such a scheme was in marked contrast to those chosen by Lady Rosina - apricot and violet, or black and gold, which were to be found at Dunbar where not only was every room refurnished and redecorated, the surplus furniture was such that it was stacked inside the hen houses and other domestic offices. Though the guiding hand was certainly Rosina's, she in collusion with her suppliers, had to ensure that the various accounts were couched in such a way as to make it seem all had been ordered by Sir Clifford in his lifetime, and therefore, that all payments became the responsibility of the estate and not herself. To secure her end, she offered no objection to overcharging, nor did she reveal the true extent of her extravagance until the year of 'election' had passed. The latter was the period during which Sir Clifford's son and heir Talbot Augustus Clifford Constable had to decide how best to stave off the near bankruptcy of the estate. During that year, by a combination of retrenchment, sales of easily realisable assets, and mortgages, it seemed just possible to prevent the sale of Burton Constable itself, which Sir Augustus vacated to live quietly at Aston House, North Ferriby.

The estate's trustees concurred, but a solicitor member of the family knew that Lady Rosina's expenses had been grossly understated. Mr. Thomas Constable pursued a policy of 'masterly inactivity' apparently because he had been socially slighted by other members of the family, but once the real truth became known, Sir Talbot was obliged to take action through the Court of Chancery in order to prevent his own bankruptcy. Henceforth it was for the Court to decide not only who had ordered what, but whether the charges could be held reasonable in the circumstances. As the case unfolded, it became clear that much had been ordered without Sir Clifford's knowledge or approval, that several of the claims were not strictly true, and that many of the charges had been inflated. Witnesses from each claimant were cross examined, and, where the account was long and complex only upon specimen items. Given that much was and still is written about Victorian morality, few of Lady Rosina's suppliers emerged with their reputations undiminished. True to family form, her commisions had been allocated to the leading men in both Hull and London, and as William Constable had discovered a century before, the Hull men at their best were equal to their London rivals, but cheaper.

The Richardsons' accounts (they were to submit three versions to the court) reveal that between an order and its delivery, a delay of fifteen months or more was possible, even without the time taken to design the item and secure approval for it. They also show that while some items were 'selected', others were 'got from Paris' or partially or wholly designed or re-designed. A few pieces were to match, for example, those already in the 'Grand Drawing Room' at Burton Constable. The new interiors were to be lit by candles, not oil or gas lamps, and were to be liberally fitted out with mirrors of every kind, and embellished with much gilding and ormoulu. The outcome was similar in effect to the interiors of those 'hotels' built by the 'grandes horizontales' in the Paris of Napoleon III, a style known to both Sir Clifford and Lady Rosina.

One consequence was that as the Richardsons were making their furniture, the more respectable gentlemen of Hull sought the Richardsons' permission to view the work in progress, such was its notoriety. One may instance the mirrored bed, or the doors faced with mirror glass, the latter bedded on india rubber pads to avoid breakage and with fittings of cut glass inset with electro-plated mounts. If the Constables' rooms glittered, their servants' room gleamed with furniture of polished birch.

The Richardsons had begun to supply Burton Constable from about 1855, that is in Lady Marianne's time, with an average annual order of about £150, but the Dunbar House commission came to about £11,000, without either Constable enquiring about the eventual cost, though insisting 'that everything was to be of the very best and I was to take Burton Constable as a Model'. Richardsons' first account failed to convince under cross-examination, and the firm produced a second, but under further cross-examination, he again admitted 'error'. Thus a cabinet and console table first charged at £98.10.0. were stated to have cost £68.9.0. When further questioned, William Richardson agreed that the real cost to him had been £41.14.6. A superior chimney glass at £42 allegedly cost £23.8.6., but its real cost was about

£16, while Richardson charged £2.2.0. each for 54 visits whereas his coachman had only recalled 29. During such visits he would discuss pattern chairs and any alterations they might need to suit the Constable taste - Sir Clifford liked to study the various plans and drawings, and both visited the shop, singly or together. During such visits to Burton Constable, Richardson was also invited to take sketches and drawings of anything he might need.

Questioned about his suppliers of fabrics, Richardson conceded that 'got from Paris' could mean goods bought from Messrs. Radleys in a French style, and the same was true of fabrics bought from Messrs. Copestake.

The Richardsons were also involved, as intermediaries, with Erards, the famous French piano makers, and with Elkingtons of Birmingham, pioneers in the manufacture of electro-plated gold and silver ware.

The first version of the Erard grand piano was intended to have cost £255, the highest price then ruling for one with an ebony and ormoulu case. Once it became clear that the piano was a personal bequest to Lady Rosina, the whole design was re-negotiated, Richardson or her Ladyship suggesting that some of the Buhlwork at Burton Constable would serve as a model. The outcome was charged at £787. . . for a piano that had not been started at Sir Clifford's death. Richardson would have got a trade commission of £42 upon the £255, but claimed he would not expect a commission for the extra decoration. Sometimes it appears that Richardson did not manufacture all his own goods. The console table charged at £98.10.0 'was partly made by White (of London) and partly by ourselves'.

A similar situation existed at the firm styled 'Le Roy' whose shop was in Regent Street. The court case shows that the famous French firm had, by 1870, become no more than a trade name that no longer had any connection with the firm's founders.

The bright colouring of their ormolu mounted porcelain clock cases complemented the 'French' tapestry covers of the chairs. In one instance, however, a Le Roy clock case forecast the Art Noveau style that only became fashionable thirty years later.

In style, Dunbar House was fashionably up-to-date and similar to the furniture then on offer from London designers such as Booths or Lawfords, the latter a reviver of Buhlwork, and, as Shoolbreds catalogue of 1881 shows, the Richardson pieces in the Louis Seize style had remained in vogue.[211]

Neither the Hull timber trade, nor the furniture making industry it serviced could be attributed to the Constables as entrepreneurs in so far as they invested their capital in either. On the other hand they were wealthy and enterprising enough to use new and fashionable materials in their building and remodelling of their house, and they gained undoubted satisfaction in the employment and encouragement of the skilled craftsmen of the locality.

These craftsmen in turn rapidly advanced their education in design and technique in manufacture as a direct result of the Constables patronage. Without the generosity of the latter, much of that progress would have been slower, if it had been made at all. Thomas Wilkinson Wallis specifically noted his gain in confidence following his early work experience for Lady Marianne, while in the late 1860's the Richardsons were able to orchestrate a surprisingly wide range of contractors to suit the plans of Lady Rosina.

In the immediate vicinity of Hull and indeed in the East Riding, the scale and extravagance of the Constables was without parallel, and as such their successive remodellings and refurnishings played a notably successful part in the development and refinement of the industry and taste of one of England's principal cities.

Many great houses can show a continuity of inheritance, but few of such continuity of design and taste.

CHAPTER SIXTEEN

EPILOGUE -
THE COLLECTIONS IN THE 20th CENTURY

In order to accommodate the new, that is the nine-teenth century furniture, some of William Constable's was sent to the attics where its discovery is commented on by the famous carver, Thomas Wilkinson Wallis in 1835. More still went to the upper part of the stable block. To this were added items from the nineteenth century refurbishment during the Edwardian restoration, the whole amounting to several hundred items. However, there was a dispersal of these surpluses in the early 1960's though it might still be possible for the whole story to be pieced together, from various inventories and auction house records. One can certainly however discern the principal elements and much of the secondary detail of each phase, which, taken together, combine to make an extraordinary story. On the one hand the Constable family's taste could be avant garde; on the other, for example the Chinese room, its creation could span sixty years (1783-c.1843), while pieces ordered from Chippendale in the 1770's were being used as models almost a century later.

30. White and gold chair by
J. and G. Carlill of Hull.

NOTES

Introduction

1. Louis Courtois and Cecil Hugh Chicester Constable, 'Jean Jacques Rouseau et William Constable', *Annales de la Societe' J.J. Rousseau*, vol.21, pp.156-76.

2. *Hull Packet*, 24 March 1812.

3. Stephen Oetterman *Das panorama die geschichte eine Massenmedium*, Frankfurt am Main, 1980.

4. William Cobbett, *Rural Rides*, London, 1912, 2 vols., p.250.

5. Isabel Burton, *The Life of Capt. Sir Richard Francis Burton*, vol.1, 1893, p.339.

The Constable Inheritance

6. An Atkinson voucher notes payments for the principal internal fittings, e.g. the altar, and for measuring the joinery work of Messrs. Taylor and Bird, and the bricklayers' work of Messrs. Milner. The surviving drawing is unsigned and not as executed.

7. The Billiard (later Coffee) Room had been designed by Atkinson in 1774 and the three tables for the niches in the apse were the work of Thomas Walker. Atkinson charged £1.1.0. per day for his services, plus travelling expenses of £1.11.6. per journey from York. The drawings 'at Large' cost Constable £5.5.0.

8. Some of the transcripts of the case are in the County Record Office, some are at Burton Constable.

Architectural development of Burton Constable

9. cf. Paull Holme Tower east of Hull.

10. The chief change was the insertion of a Gothic revival window in the north wall, glazed with stained glass of both the Georgian and Victorian periods.

11. The very detailed late seventeenth century painting of the house and adjacent park hangs in the Great Hall.

12. This part of the north front was marked by a huge beech tree. The topmost storey is still internally unfinished.

13. See the painting noted at (6) above.

14. A similar Adam ceiling was executed for Sir Watkin Williams - Wynn's house at 20 St. James Square and illustrated in colour in Adam's *Works in Architecture*, a copy of which remains, still in its original parts and wrappers at Burton Constable.

15. Brown's scheme for the Hall ceiling was later adapted for use at Corsham Court, Wiltshire.

16. Lightoler's presentation for Burton Constable drawings include many carefully coloured to heighten their realism and are evidence that Lightoler tried hard to win Constable's favour.

17. See Dr. Norman Higson, *Transactions of the Georgain Society for East Yorkshire*, Vol.V part II, 1961-63, pp.41-54 - where the building history is treated in full. The project took ten years to complete.

William Constable - his ideas and ideals

18. Hannah Williamson left the Constables on their Grand Tour, in 1770 after 14 years service, to marry an Irish footman. Nevertheless William Constable granted her an annuity; Vol.37, (Vol.2), 1769-1770, France and Italy p.32.

19. He wrote this to Messrs. Jeffries and Jones, Nov. 15th 1789.
    C.N. Cochin and J.C. Bellicard *Observations sur les antiquities de la Ville d'Herculaneum*, Paris, 1754.

20. Constable ordered seventeen 'volumes' of Piranese's engravings during his third Grand Tour.

21. Piranesi dedicated plate 38 . . . of his *Vasi e Candelabri* to William Constable while the jambs of the chimney pieces shown on pls.38 and 22 of Piranesi's *Diversi maniere d'adornare i camini* are the models for the final design of the Wyatt/Bacon chimney piece for the Great Drawing Room devised to celebrate Constable's marriage in 1775. The book was published in Rome in 1769. The main frieze is an adapation of the Antique Roman painting, the Aldobrandini Marriage, a coloured print of which James Byres was to send to Constable.

22. Sir Christopher Sykes was to do the same during his reconstruction of Sledmere in the 1780's.

23. This would have been where Wyatt's drawing room is now i.e. as far away as possible from the kitchen.

24. Perhaps the first Roman revival interior is that at Packington Hall of the 1780's, designed by the Earl of Aylesford and Joseph Bonomi.

25. e.g. Common place Notebooks, 'Vol.1 transcribed'.

26. See I. Hall, 'A Yorkshireman with Roman tastes', *Country Life*, Jan. 27, 1977, p.220-221.

27. Mark Catesby (1683-1749), illustrated the rattlesnake in his *Natural History of Carolina*, London, 1730-48, pl.41.

28. Robert Constable is said to have joined the Crusade of 1189 and died abroad.

The Cabinet of scientific instruments

29. Catholic Record Society: Series, *The Douai College Diaries* 7th Diary, 1715-78, p.213; Catholic Record Society Record Series *Douai College Documents* Vol.63 (1972) p.120.

30. H.C.R.O. DDCC 140, 1742.

31. H.C.R.O. DDCC 144/9.

32. Bodleian Library. MS. English letters 229 p.126. These ms. form the only sizeable collection of the Burton Constable archive so far discovered, separated from the archive deposited at the Humberside Record office. They consist of some of the most valuable letters and accounts concerning William Constable.

33. G.L.'E. Turner, 'The cabinet of experimental philosophy', *The Origins of Museums* (ed. Impey and MacGregor), 1985, pp.214-22. Turner discusses the interplay between aristocratic patron and instrument maker and its positive effect on the advancement of science from the 15th to the 18th century. See also A. McCann, 'A private laboratory at Petworth House, Sussex, in the late eighteenth century', *Annals of Science*, Vol.40, 1983, pp.635-655.

34. Douglas McKie, 'Priestley's laboratory and library and other of his effects', *Notes and records* XII, 1956, pp.114-136.

35. A list of apparatus belonging to the itinerant lecturer Adam Walker (1731-1821) which was to be put on display prior to a lecture in York, occurs in the *York Courant*, 24 March 1772.

36. Musson and Robinson, *Science and Technology in the Industrial Revolution*, 1970, p.102.

37. Arden is known to have lived in Beverley intermittently from 1756. He became freeman there in 1758 when described as 'phylosopher'. See Humberside County Record Office BC/IV/7/1. His

sons, James and John were apprenticed to their father in 1767 and 1768 respectively and James was to help his father with his experiments later becoming surgeon at Howden. See also A.J. Turner, *Music and Science in 18th Century Bath*, Exhib. cat., 1979, p.83.

38. University Library, Cambridge, 58 . . . 802.

39. In commonplace notebook 'Wycliffe Mr. T' Burton Constable Muniments.

40. See note 32.

41. Unless otherwise indicated the vouchers that document the apparatus are at the Humberside County Record Office (H.C.R.O.) under DDCC (2), in various numbered boxes according to date. Box 48 for 1755-7 is *48*, 1758-61 is *49*, 1761-63 is *50*, 1764-66 is *51*, 1767-69 is *52*, 1770-72 is *53*, 1773-75 is *54*, 1776-78 is *55*, 1779-81 is *56*, 1782-84 is *57*, 1785-86 is *58*, 1787-88 is *59*, 1789-93 is *60*.

42. W.D. Hackmann, *Electricity from Glass*, 1978, p.111. B. Wilson; *Treatise on Electricity*, 1750, Fig.1. p.4 is reproduced by Hackmann.

43. British Library M.S. 4440 (617). The letter is printed in full by A.J. Turner *op.cit.*, note.7.

44. Hackmann, *op.cit.*, p.107.

45. For the history of the Cole and Adam firm-see: E.G.R. Taylor, *Mathematical Practitioners in Hanoverian England*, 1966, pp.199-200 and p.152. Many Adam instruments are in the George 3 collection in the Science Museum.

46. DDCC 145/1. Included in an account sent by John Dunn on May 17th 1767 is 'To Mr. Adams Elect. Machine etc. as per Bill'.

47. Edward Nairne, *Directions for using the electrical machine* London, 1773.

48. I. Hall *William Constable as Patron*, Exhibition Catalogue. Ferens Art Gallery, Hull, 1970, p.6.

49. *D.N.B.*, Vol.V, p.1102.

50. Bodleian Library, M.S. English Letts. C.229, p.117. In 1769 Thomas Pennant purchased an 'astronomcial instrument 'from Mr. Hinley' along with a 'Portbl. Telescope', maker unstated, for £10.10. The latter may be the portable Ramsden telescope mentioned above.

51. We are grateful to members of staff of the Science Museum and the British Library for helping us with the identification of the paper and board items.

52. Joseph Moxon (1627-1700) Printer, author and instrument maker. He only produced paper and board instruments, the scales and lines being printed on the paper shown on a published plate by T. Tuttell; E.G.R. Taylor *Mathematical practitioners of Tudor and Stuart England*, pp.234-5.

53. George Adams (1704-73) included a mention of his new invention on the title page of *Micrographia Illustrata*, 1771.

54. Robert Smith, *A Compleat System of Opticks*, 1738, Fig.635.

55. Coles instruction for use, with advice on looking 'at perspectives' is separated from the account and found in Bodleian M.S. English letters C.227, p.112.

56. John Arden, *Syllabus for lectures in experimental philosophy*, Beverley, 1772.

57. Thanks to John Hammond and staff of the History of Science Museum, Oxford, for help in identification.

58. The Adams waywiser is in full working order.

59. John R. Milburn, *Annals of Science*, 1983, p.447, and *Wheelwright of the Heavens*, 1988, p.274.

60. H.C.R.O. DDCC 145/1.

61. W.A. Mozart *Adagio for glass harmonica*, K.356 and 619. Information from the late Dr. D. Rushman.

62. Joseph Priestley *Memoirs* 4th ed. (1833) p.63.

63. Bodleian Library M.S. English Letters C.229, p.141.

64. The mirror, focal length 56 inches, took 15 minutes to set a piece of paper alight.

65. J. Priestley, *Experiments and observations on different kinds of air*, Vol.II, pp.293-303 and pl.III, p.302.

66. H.C.R.O. DDCC Box.49. On a mid 18th century trade card Adams advertises his willingness to make models to order - *Annals of science*, Vol.42, 1985, p.472.

67. H.C.R.O. DDCC 145/1-4.

68. G.L.'E. Turner, 'A goodly huge cabinet', *Annals of science*, Vol.41, 1984, p.169 (review).

Natural History - the herbarium

69. J. Britten, *The Sloane herbarium*, The British Museum, 1958, edited and revised by J.E. Dandy. See also D.H. Kent, *British Herbaria*, British Museum (Natural History) 1987 and second edition.

70. The herbarium is kept in the Library closet at Burton Constable. It has recently been catalogued.

71. 'Eleven drawings of plants, framed' - in the entry for the north wing 'Heirlooms' 1791. (uncatalogued) at the house. Ehret charged for a number of drawings at various times.

72. Carl Linnaeus, *Philosophia botanica*, no.11, 1751.

73. Wilfred Blunt *The compleat naturalist*, London (1971) W.T. Stearn appendix p.244.

74. W.T. Stearn Introduction *Species plantarum* Facs. London, 1957, p.75.
    See also F.A. Stafleu, *Linnaeus and the Linnaeans - The spreading of their ideas in systematic botany*, Utrecht, 1971.

75. D.E. Allen, *The Naturalist in Britain*, p.40.

76. *Hortus Cliffortianus* is listed in the 1775 catalogue of the Library closet.

77. H.C.R.O. DDCC 145/2.

78. Ed. G.S. Rousseau, *The letters and papers of Sir John Hill 1714-1775*.

79. J.J. Rousseau, *Letter on the elements of botany addressed to a lady*, reprint Michael Joseph 1979, p.114.

80. A. Royen *Flora Leydensis*, 1740; the specimen in question has been identified as *Coreopsis tuptens*.

81. Henrey (Knowlton) *op.cit.* p.121.

82. *Garden History*, vol.14, no.1, p.27. A catalogue of Gray's nursery dated 1755 is at the Lindley library. See Blanche Henrey, *British botanical literature before 1800*, Oxford, 1975, p.49.

83. John Dunn's correspondence H.C.R.O. DDCC 145/2.

84. William Darlington, *Memorials of John Bartram and Humphrey Marshall*, Philadelphia, 1849.

85. Elizabeth Maclean, *An eighteenth century herbarium at the Sutro Library California*, A State library foundation bulletin, 6 Jan. 1984. See also Hilda Grieve, *A transatlantic gardening friendship*, Historical Assoc., Essex branch, 1980.

86. *Garden history*, vol.14, pp.20 and 24.

87. Wilfred Blunt, *The compleat naturalist* Appendix W.T. Stearn, p.242.

88. In the Herbarium, British Museum (Natural History).

89. DDCC 145/6. James Byres to William Constable.

90. A pencil survey drawn before Brown's improvements had been started has recently been discovered at Burton Constable.

91. Robert Teesdale, 'Plantae Eboracense', *Transactions of the Linnaean Society*, 5, supplement, 1800, pp.36-93. Teesdale was assisted by Colonel Machell, who also helped to prepare the list in G. Poulson, *Beverlac*, Beverley (1831).

92. E. Crackles, *Flora of the East Riding of Yorkshire*, Hull University 1990 e.g.p. 90. There is no mention of Constable's records in this wide ranging and thorough survey.

93. F.H. Perring and S.M. Walters, *Atlas of the British Flora*, p.166.

94. Blanche Henrey, (Knowlton) *op.cit.* There are many entries concerning the plants Knowlton sought and grew.

95. B. Henrey, (Knowlton), p.257.

96. See sale catalogue *John Fothergill collection*, August 1781, p.37; Lot 31 - 23 pots including *Erinus alpinus, Alyssum alpinus, Linnea borealis*. [British Library B.95 (4)].

97. Mea Allen, *William Robinson 1838-1935*, London, 1982, p.29. William Robinson was enthusiastic about Niven's large collection in 1863.

98. Philip Miller, *The gardener's dictionary*, 6th ed. 1752, (abridged), Cramer reprint, 1969, p.623. John Fothergill grew this orchid at his garden in Upton. (Sale catalogue p.8).

99. Jean O'Neill. 'Plants for an intire stranger' *Country Life*, 21 May 1981.

100. *Op.cit.* note 3, p.214.

101. See also D.E. Allen, *op.cit.* p.40.

102. For example Hull botanic garden was founded in 1812.

William Constable 'Fossil Cabinet'

103. Henry Baker (1698-1774), naturalist and poet, a fellow of the Society of Antiquaries, elected 1740, the same year as he became a Fellow of the Royal Society. Awarded Copley medal for microscopic experiments on saline crystallisation, author of 'The Microscope made easy' 1743, and 'Employment for the Microscope', 1753. Responsible for the introduction of the alpine strawberry and the rhubarb plant. An extensive natural history and antiquarian collection was sold after his death.

104. Thomas Pennant (1726-1798). A correspondent of Linnaeus and was made a member of the Royal Society of Uppsala in 1757 at his instigation; elected Fellow of the Royal Society 1767. Author of *The British Zoology* 1766; *A tour in Scotland*, 1769; *Synopsis of Quadrupeds*, 1771; *A tour in Wales* 1770, etc.

105. Fox, R.D., *Dr. John Fothergill and his friends Chapters in eighteenth century life*, London, 1919.

106. Whitehead, P.J.P. 'Emanuel Mendes da Costa (1719-91) and the *Conchology or Natural History of Shells*', *Bulletin of the British Museum (Natural History), Historical Series*, vol.6 (1) 1977, pp. 1-24.

107. Boyd, M.J. and Credland, A.G., 'Hippocephaloides of Dr. Plot; or how one thing leads to another', *Geological Curator*, vol.4, 1984, pp.43-4.

108. Allen, D.E. *The Naturalist in Britain : a social*

history, London, 1976.

William Constables zoological collection

109. The parterre was damaged in transit (letter from Emanuel da Costa apologises for this, 30 December 1760). There is no indication it was returned by Constable so the surviving example is presumable the same piece repaired and reassembled.

110. *Annals of Science*, vol.43, 1986, pp.147-174. The surviving artefacts suggest a display along the traditional lines, if not in the extravagance, shown in the surviving drawings. See also O. Impey and A. MacGregor ed. *The origins of Museums*, 1985.

111. H.C.R.O. DDCC 145/1-3.

112. The ornamental heading of the catalogue depicts a series of orangery type buildings set in a garden of rectangular flower beds, enlivened by various creatures including peacocks and a dog. Brookes advertises that 'quadrupeds of all sorts are exchanged' and animals conveyed 'to all parts of the world'.

113. For an account of the content of contemporary menageries see Sally Festing. *Journal of Garden History* vol.8, no.4, Oct./Dec. 1989.

The gun cabinet and the Wallis workshop

114. W. Keith Neal and D.H.L. Back, *Great British Gunmakers 1740-90*, London, 1975; pp. 87-98 and numerous illustrations.

115. The Burton Constable archive is preserved at the County Record Office, Beverley.

116. W. Keith Neal, 'A sporting gun from the cabinet of Burton Constable', *Arms and Armour at the Dorchester*, London, 1982.
See also Guy Wilson 'Britain's most expensive gun', *Shooting Times and Country Magazine*, May 4-10, 1989, pp.24-5.

117. *Hull City Archives, Bench Book 9, 14 March 1743.*

118. Hull City Archives BRF6/725; BRF/6773; BRF6/780, etc. He died in 1778.

119. A.G. Credland, 'Wallis of Hull' *The Journal of the Arms and Armour Society*, Vol.9, no.4, Dec. 1978, pp. 133-185.

120. See 1791 directory; ironmonger in Market place, Sinkler and Bell, smiths of Quay Street, dock side. The pistol was sold at Christies as lot 208 'Important Firearms, Arms and Armour', 13 Dec. 1966. In 1783 a receipt dated 7 January of George Sinkler, cutler, lists a variety of locks, screws, shovels and pack thread costing £9.7s.6d.

121. See 'Wallis of Hull' *op.cit.* pp. 138-9.

122. A.G. Credland, 'George Wallis, the younger, gunsmith of Mytongate, Hull', *Guns Review*, April 1988, vol.28, no.4, pp.292-3.

123. See 'Wallis of Hull' *op.cit.* pp.141-3.

124. A single loose sheet which has become displaced from the bundles of accounts and still remains at Burton Constable Hall.

125. A.G. Credland 'Silver Street, Hull' *Guns Review*, Nov. 1989, vol.29, no.11, pp.852-3.
The premises were briefly occupied, 1833-5 by John Blanch Jnr, son of the eminent London gunmaker of the same name. He billed a Mr. Charles Phillips, evidently a guest at Burton Constable, for powder and percussion caps (24 January 1834). Mozeen evidently retired owing to ill health and died a year later aged only fifty.

126. A.G. Credland 'Silver Street, Hull, William Needler (and son) 1845-95' *Guns Review*, March 1990, vol.30, no.3, pp.188-9. Needler died 7 June 1882.

The Wallis museum,
its inspirations and contemporaries

127. W.J. Smith, 'The life and activities of Sir Ashton Lever of Alkrington, 1729-88', *Transactions of the Lancashire and Cheshire antiquarian society*, vol.72, 1962, pp.61-92.

128. Richard Altick, *The Shows of London*, London, 1978 pp.28-32 etc.

129. For the most up-to-date assessment see Edmund P. Alexander 'William Bullock : Little-remembered museologist and showman', *Curator*, Vol.28, no.2, 1985, pp.117-147.

130. George Hadley, *A New and Complete History of Kingston upon Hull*, 1788, pp.401-2.

131. Sword fish.

132. Narwhal; an Arctic whale.
During the Middle Ages the horn was thought to be the horn of a fabulous creature, partaking of the characteristics of an antelope and a horse, and was greatly sought after by Kings and princes throughout Europe. Huge sums of money were paid for the unicorn's horn, shavings of which were supposed to provide an antidote to poison when added to wine or food.

133. Walrus.

134. Rev. John Tickell, *History of the Town and County of Kingston upon Hull*, 1798, p.842.

135. Claude Blair, A royal swordsmith and damascener - Diego de Caias' *Metropolitan Museum Journal*, New York, vol.3, 1970, pp.149-198.

136. Richard Greene, *A Particular and descriptive catalogue of the natural and artificial rarities in the Lichfield Museum*, 1782.

137. T. Gibbon, 'Thomas Barrit of Manchester - a memoir', *Reliquary; quarterly archaelogical review*, vol.9, 1868-9.

138. *Ancient arms and weapons in the possession of Thomas Barrit*, 1793; archive department, central library, Manchester.

139. J.F. Earwaker, 'On certain swords inscribed *Edwardus Prins Anglie'*, *Archaeological Journal*, vol.30, March 1873.

140. A.G. Credland, 'Wallis of Hull' *The Journal of the Arms and Armour Society*, vol.9, no.4, December, 1979, pp.133-185.

141. *Hull Packet*, 9 September 1800.

142. Broadsheet in private collection.

143. *Hull Packet*, 15 September 1807.

144. *Hull Packet*; advertisements appeared almost every week from September to November.

145. The collection was housed at 22 Piccadilly occupying part of the site of what became Swan and Edgar's department store. In 1812 a new building was erected on the south side of Piccadilly nearly opposite the end of Bond Street. The mock ancient facade gave it the popular name of the Egyptian hall, a favourite resort for the curious for many years though Bullocks own museum collection was sold off in 1819 in an auction lasting nine days.

146. *Catalogue of a museum consisting of ancient and modern arms and armour etc. originally collected by the late Mr. Wallis, an eminent gunsmith in Hull*, 1833, 54 pp.

147. John Craggs, *A new guide to Hull*, Hull, 1836, pp.55-6.

148. Though the society may not have acted as a body to acquire the contents of the museum, certain items including the Armathwaite sword were purchased by its members, See Earwaker, note *supra*.

149. R.W. Fairholt and R. Wright *Miscellanea*

graphica - representations of ancient, medieval and renaissance remains in the possession of Lord Londesborough, London, 1856, see pl.27.

150. Sale catalogue of 1833, cat.no.146, museum no.233.

151. *ibid* cat.no.176, museum no.370; it had two turn-over barrels mounted one above the other.

152. Major General Ralph Burton, Colonel of the 3rd Foot, commander of the British forces in Canada and Lieutenant Governor of Quebec. Born 1725, son of Richard Burton of Hull Bank House, he died 24 September 1768 and is memorialised in Cottingham Parish Church.

153. Sale catalogue of 1833; cat.no.207, museum no.81; Tower Armouries inv.no.IX.764.

154. *Dictionary of National Biography*; Josef Boruwlaski (ed. H.R. Hartley) *The Life and Love Letters of a dwarf*, London, 1902.

155. *Hull Packet*, 17 May and 24 June, 1803. He retired to Durham where he died in 1837 aged 98 and was buried in the cathedral under a tablet simply inscribed JB.

156. A note in the Burton Constable archives refers to the London residence and *packaging up the museum*, in October 1782; see also DDCC (2) 57 which refers to installation of a skylight in the museum.

157. A marked catalogue of the sale is preserved by Messrs. Christies, London.

158. Many of Tunstall's books being purchased by a Mr. Todd a bookseller of York.

159. George Allan (1736-1800), lawyer and antiquary, was a friend of Tunstall's.

160. Following his death, 18 May 1800, Allan's collections were brought from the executors by his son. In June 1822 the latter decided to sell the museum by public auction but following an approach from George Townshead Fox of the Literary and Philosophical Society of Newcastle upon Tyne agreed to let them have the whole contents for £400.
The museum was arranged in the society's rooms and was a major inspiration behind the formation in 1829 of the Natural History Society of Northumberland, Durham and Newcastle upon Tyne. The Allan museum as it became known formed the nucleus around which the present Hancock museum was established.

161. G.T. Fox *Synopsis of the Newcastle Museum, late the Allan, formerly the Tunstall and Wycliffe Museum*, Newcastle, 1827, p.179, etc.

162. He opened his museum in 1778 at Great Yarmouth. It contained specimens from Lever, Sir Astley Cooper, the royal surgeon, and included 118 Cook artefacts. The collection was dismantled after Boulter's death in 1802.

163. George Humphreys of St. Martins Lane, London, dispersed one large collection in April 1779 and a second was sold to the University of Gottingen, Germany, in 1782. The latter is now the largest identifiable and best preserved Cook voyage collection which has survived.

164. Warner Dawson, editor, *The Banks letters*, London, 1958, p.772.

165. Sale catalogue of 1833.

166. E.J. Heseltine, *Catalogue of pictures, engravings, furniture and objects of interest in the Trinity House, Hull*, 1928.

**Constable the improver -
the creation of a landscape garden**

167. Bodleian Library M.S. Eng. Letters 229 p.218.

168. *Garden History*, Vol.14, no.1, p.7.

169. The known accounts for this Brown commission are fragmentary. In Brown's account book at the R.H.S. (Lindley) Library i.e. for the bridge and a painting by Clerisseau. The voucher bundles DDCC (2) box 52 show a receipt from Mr. Brown for £8.4.

170. *Garden History*, vol.14, p.10 and 12 show some Lightoler designs.

171. Dorothy Stroud *Capability Brown*, 2nd ed. 1975, p.173. Stroud discusses the Brown visits of 1773, 1779 and 1778.

172. Trenches are still visible round some of the clumps, particularly either side of the Marton Road on East Lawn.

173. The voucher bundles concerning Brown's improvements are to be found at H.C.R.O. DDCC (2) boxes 52.57.

174. The nurserymans accounts can be found at H.C.R.O. DDCC (2) boxes 53-60.

175. The present Engine House was certainly remodelled for Sir Clifford Constable.

176. It has been suggested by Michael Charlesworth that the later Brown style with its simpler less symbolic features, is paralleled in the changing attitudes to literature shown by authors such as Fielding and Richardson.

The Library

177. Burton Constable muniments. The 1775 catalogue and the 'Heirlooms' list are among the Burton Constable muniments at the house.

178. H.C.R.O. DDCC 140/1 Nov. 1743.

179. Benjamin White was a bookseller and publisher with a particular interest in natural history. He was brother to the famous naturalist Gilbert and friend of William Curtis, sharing in the venture of Curtis's first botanic garden in 1771.

180. Alan Stevenson *A bibliographical study of William Curtis 'Flora Londinensis', 1778-98*, MacMasters Millan Hunt Foundation, 1961. The plates were intended to be put together by the purchaser according to the Linaean system. By making an alphabetical index employing common names, Constable may have had other users such as his gardener in mind. The indexing of the plates has remained a bibliographical problem.

A century of Constable patronage

181. Hargrave's detail is richer than that shown on Wyatt's drawings.

182. e.g. 'Horseshoe table making 48 days, writing desk making 58 days at 2/- per day.'

183. Joseph Hargrave became an architect. The engraved plates sponsored by Constable for Dade's projected 'History of Holderness', include one by Hargrave of Grimston Garth, a house designed by John Carr.

184. Thomas Wilkinson Wallis, *Autobiography*, Louth 1899.

The Burton Constable whale

185. Drogo de Bevere was the first Lord of the Seignory and was granted the territory by William the Conqueror whose expedition he had accompanied. It remained a single territorial unit throughout the Middle Ages, reverted to the crown in 1293 and was thereafter held by a succession of Crown grantees. The territory reverted to the crown in 1521 with the execution and attainder of the Duke of Buckingham.

186. J.L. Drury 'The Bishop of Durham's Whale' *Bulletin of the Durham County Local History Society*, 25 December 1980, pp.39-52.

187. A lesser rorqual (piked or minke whale) washed up on the Holderness coast, in 1828 was prepared by the Rev. Christopher Sykes and John

Phillips, the noted geologist, and for a time was displayed at Sledmere Hall (E. Yorks) evidently a rival to the Burton Constable whale. Only the skull survives, preserved in the Yorkshire Museum, York. More recently another piked whale was stranded between Hilston and Tunstall, July 1982, the skull is now in the Town Docks Museum. In January 1985 some thirty pilot whales came ashore between Holmpton and Easington. The most recent stranding of a sperm whale in the vicinity of the Humber was in 1976 when a male animal, 49 foot long was washed up at Skidbrooke on the Lincolnshire coast.

188. James Alderson (1794-1882) born in Hull the younger son of Dr. John Alderson, entered Pembroke College, Oxford, in 1818 and gained his BA degree four years later. Made an MA in 1825 he was incorporated at Magdalen Hall, Oxford, as MB and the degree of M.D. followed in 1829. Admitted a candidate of the College of Physicians in 1826 he was made a fellow in 1830. For a short time he was physician to the Carey Street dispensary in London but succeeded to his father's large and lucrative practice in Hull, the East Riding and Lincolnshire. Alderson was elected physician to the Royal Infirmary and remained in the city until 1851.

189. A copy is preserved at Burton Constable Hall.

190. An example is in the collections of the Town Docks Museum, Hull.

191. James Alderson 'An account of a whale of the Spermaceti tribe cast on the Yorkshire coast on the 28 April 1825' *Transactions of the Cambridge Philosophical Society*, 1827, pp.253-66. Alderson was a member of the society. The *Annual Report of the Yorkshire Philosophical Society*, 1827 (published 1828) records that a Mr. G. Sawyer presented portions of the aorta and heart of the whale.

192. I am indebted to John Chichester Constable for bringing this volume to my attention.

193. Print in the Town Docks Museum, Hull.

194. John Evelyn, *Diary of John Evelyn*, ed. E.S. de Beer, Oxford 1955, 6 vols.

195. John Hunter, 'Observations on the structure and economy of whales' *Philosophical Transactions*, vol.77, 1787, pp.371-450.

196. Thomas Beale (1807-49) was a student at the Aldersgate medical school 1827-9 and stayed on as assistant in the dissecting room and later as assistant curator. He moved to the London hospital in the same capacity but was determined to travel and take part in a whaling voyage to the South Seas. In 1830 Beale sailed as a surgeon aboard the whaleship *Kent* belonging to Thomas Sturge, friend of Macaulay the historian. During the voyage he exchanged berths with the surgeon of the *Sarah and Elizabeth*, another of Sturges vessels, seeking a commander more sympathetic to his interests. Back in England he was awarded the silver medal of the Eclectic Society of London for a paper he gave concerning *Physeter mocrocephalus*, the Sperm whale. Beale took a post as assistant surgeon of St. John's British Hospital, Hatton Gardens, London, and for ten years was medical assistant to the Royal Humane Society. Elected MRCS in 1841 and medical officer to the Stepney Poor House in 1842 he died there on 22 August 1849, aged only 42, during the great cholera epidemic.

197. Surgeon and lecturer in anatomy and physiology of the Hull and East Riding School of Anatomy and Medicine established in 1831 by Dr. James Alderson, R. Craven, R. Harvey and Wallis himself. He was the son of an Edward Wallis who was initially a joiner then was employed as a commercial traveller by Crackles and Horncastle, whalebone manufacturers who later

took him into partnership. See the *Autobiography of Thomas Wilkinson Wallis*, Hull, 1899, he gives a brief family history and refers to Surgeon Wallis as his cousin. At the end of James Aldersons account of the whale, read in 1825 (see note 191) he stated that 'the skeleton will be articulated and preserved at Burton Constable' and that 'The bones are now macerating in pits, where they will have to remain a considerable time. In the Autumn, probably the process of articulating will be commenced . . .'

198. Sir Thomas Aston Clifford Constable (1807-70), second baronet.

199. The book was also an inspiration to J.M.W. Turner, who painted four canvases with whaling themes, one at least of which was commissioned by Elhanan Bicknell (1788-1861), a patron of the arts and whaling entrepreneur of Newington Butts, and the remainder executed with him in mind. Two were exhibited as *'Whalers'* at the Royal Academy in 1845 and *Hurrah for the Whaler Erebus! another fish* and *Whalers (boiling blubber) entangled in flaw ice, endeavouring to extricate themselves* in 1846 (See M. Butlin and E. Jolly *The Paintings of J.M.W. Turner*, 1984 nos. 414, 415, 423, 426). Three of the works when exhibited at the R.A. had references to Beale's (1839) account of his voyage appended to the title and relate to dramatic incidents described by him in the pursuit of the whale.
Bicknell subscribed to four copies of Beales volume and the firm of Bicknell and Langton commissioned the marine artist W.J. Huggins to paint two canvases of whalers in which they held an interest. The design of one of these has a close relationship to the whaling scene now in the Metropolitan Museum, New York, by Turner who seems to have used it as the basis for his own painting. Huggins also seems to be the source of the drawings on which the vignettes

and plates in Beale's book derive and the latter's patron, Thomas Sturge, whaleship owner, was also a resident of Newington Butts which points to an intimate relationship between these various artists and patrons (Correspondence with Mr. Peter Bicknell, 1985).

200. Herman Melville, *Moby Dick*, 1967 (Norton Critical Edition) chapter 102, pp.375-6. The novel was first published in America and England in 1851.

201. The remains lie some 500 yards south-east of the hall alongside the South Walk in the area called the Whale Belt; an obelisk nearby is a useful indicator.

202. It may be noted that the Assembly Rooms and the medical school where Edward Wallis taught faced one another on opposite sides of Kingston Square. The Hull Literary and Philosophical Society was formed in 1821 and the museum the following year though it was not housed in the Assembly Rooms until 1831. The prime mover behind the society was Dr. John Alderson MD (1758-1829) the father of James Alderson. Born at Lowestoft the son of a dissenting minister he settled in Hull after completing his training as a doctor and in 1795 was elected physician to the Hull Infirmary, founded 1782. A statue was erected in his memory outside the hospital in 1833 and was transferred to the present Hull Royal Infirmary which opened in 1967.

203. J.E. Gray FRS 'On the Finner whales with the description of a new species' *Proceedings of the Zoological Society of London*, 1867 esp pp.92-3. Gray received his description of the blue whale skeleton from Mr. Pearsall curator of the Lit. and Phil. Museum.

204. See Thomas Sheppard 'Notes on the skeleton of the Sibbald's Rorqual in the Hull Museum' *The Naturalist*, August 1901, pp.173-4. Reprinted

the same year as the first in a long series of Hull Museums Publications. Sheppard was the first curator of the municipal museum.

205. Thomas Sheppard, 'The Sibbald's Rorqual of the Hull Museum, *The Naturalist*, 1 May, 1935, p.188. The move was encouraged by Sir Alister Clavering Hardy MA, BSc (Oxon), FRS, FLS, FRGS, FZS as he was to become; born 1896, died 1985. He was then the professor of the department of zoology which he had established at the University College of Hull and had charge of for fourteen years during which time he under took fundamental research into the feeding habits of fish.

**Sir Clifford Constable his first wife
Lady Marianne and their furniture**

206. Thomas Wilkinson Wallis *op.cit.* p.36 'I shall have no one to depend upon but you'.

207. Thomas Wilkinson Wallis *op.cit.* p.51.

208. J.B. Waring *Masterpieces of Industrial Art and sculpture at the International Exhibition 1862*, Day & Son, 1863, pl.137.

209. Most standard works omit any reference to Hull as a furniture making centre, whilst acknowledging its shortlived pottery industry.

210. George Poulson *The History and Antiquities of the Seignory of Holderness* Hull, R. Brown, 1841, Vol.II.
The house is described on pp.242-249; the Boudoir on p.246.

211. cf. the comparative plates of *'Pictorial Directory of British 19th century Furniture Design'*, intro. by Edward Joy, Antique Collectors Club, Woodbridge, Suffolk, 1977.